FZ88
A VISUAL DOCUMENTARY
ZAPPA'S FINAL TOUR

FZ88
A VISUAL DOCUMENTARY
ZAPPA'S FINAL TOUR

Photos by Sergio "Milo" Albonico
Words by Andrew Greenaway

WP
WYMER
PUBLISHING
Bedford, England

First published in Great Britain in 2019
by Wymer Publishing
www.wymerpublishing.co.uk
Tel: 01234 326691
Wymer Publishing is a trading name of Wymer (UK) Ltd

Copyright © 2019 Wymer Publishing.
This edition published 2021.

ISBN: 978-1-912782-74-1

The Author hereby asserts his rights to be identified
as the author of this work in accordance with sections
77 to 78 of the Copyright, Designs & Patents Act 1988.

All rights reserved. No part of this publication may be
reproduced or transmitted in any form or by any means,
electronic or mechanical, including photocopying, or any
information storage and retrieval system, without written
permission from the publisher.

This publication is sold subject to the condition that it shall not,
by way of trade or otherwise, be lent, re-sold, hired out or
otherwise circulated without the publishers prior consent in any
form of binding or cover other than that in which it is published
and without a similar condition including this condition
being imposed on the subsequent purchaser.

Every effort has been made to trace the copyright holders of the
photographs in this book but some were unreachable. We would
be grateful if the photographers concerned would contact us.

Typeset and Design by Andy Bishop / 1016 Sarpsborg
Printed and bound in England by Halstan Ltd.

A catalogue record for this book is available from the British Library.

Cover design by 1016 Sarpsborg
Front cover photo © Milo Albonico
Back cover photo © Milo Albonico

INTRODUCTION

This collection is intended to complement *Zappa The Hard Way* — my book on Frank Zappa's world tour of 1988. While my earlier tome was not a definitive account of the tour, coupled together with this visual documentary (replete with new quotes from those involved), it's now almost certainly the closest we'll ever get to one.

The 'Broadway The Hard Way' tour (as Frank named it) turned out to be his last. It featured a 12-piece band with a repertoire of over 100 songs. Sadly, it ended prematurely and in disarray, with Zappa claiming to have lost $400,000 as a result.

Although he referred to it as a world tour, 'Broadway The Hard Way' in fact played to audiences on the East Coast of the United States and Europe only. Frank talked of having to cancel West Coast dates, but when I approached band members about this, none had seen anything to verify this. Indeed, drummer Chad Wackerman went so far as to tell me, *"I'll save you some time on researching this. Nothing was booked beyond the dates that we played. It was an idea to possibly add more, so nothing was cancelled."*

Twenty years after the tour collapsed, Frank's widow Gail said, *"Frank asked each SIDEMAN in the band if they would continue to tour with [bassist] Scott Thunes. What this means is that he gave everyone a fair shot at self-determining if they would be what he had hired them to be and what he was paying them to be — professional musicians. They all declined save Mike Keneally and Scott. Professional musicians: there to do a job and do it correctly — irrespective of the challenges and obstacles that may from time to time present themselves. It was sheer mutiny."* [i]

Frank himself said, *"I couldn't replace Scott to assuage everybody in the band who hated him. There's no bass player who could have done that job. The repertoire was so large, the workings of the show so complex, you had to know so much — there was no way. I pay people to rehearse, so in order to change anybody, I would have to rent a sound stage, which is $2000 a day, stick the band in there and pay them to learn to live with another bass player. And I would resist doing that simply because I don't like the idea of having a whole band ganging up on me, forcing me to get rid of a bass player I liked."* [ii]

Despite this premature end to his touring life, 'Broadway The Hard Way' is exceedingly well documented — both by Frank and, after his passing (on December 4, 1993), his family — through various officially released audio recordings. A full 1988 discography can be found elsewhere in this book.

In the near ten years since I wrote *Zappa The Hard Way*, Frank's eldest son Dweezil (guitar) has continued to perform his father's music worldwide. His group has mutated into what he today calls the best band he's ever assembled. Only Scheila Gonzalez (brass/woodwinds/keyboards) remains from Dweezil's original line-up of an ensemble that for ten years toured under the 'Zappa Plays Zappa' banner. This all changed on October 7, 2015 when Gail Zappa passed away.

In July 2015, knowing the end was nigh, Gail partnered with Universal Music Enterprises (UMe) for a long-term, global licensing agreement for Frank's entire recorded catalogue and announced that their youngest son, Ahmet, would *"be taking over the daily operations of the family business."* [iii]

When she passed away a few months later, control of the Zappa Family Trust (ZFT) passed to the two youngest Zappa children, Ahmet and Diva. Dweezil and his older sister Moon were not trustees, but all four children were beneficiaries. Dweezil then wrote an open letter to his brother revealing, *"Moon and I have a 20% share each of the ZFT and you and Diva have 30% each. This was deliberately created to be unequal by our mother."* He further claimed his mother had run *"the business into the ground, spent $20 million in lawsuits and by her demise was $6 million in debt."* [iv]

Several months of public animosity ensued, with Dweezil setting up a crowdfunding campaign to help fund his legal costs while fighting his siblings' attempts to register his surname — which he felt meant he could no longer go out on tour as Zappa Plays Zappa. 130% of an unspecified goal was raised and then, in May 2018, he announced that he had gotten together with Diva and Ahmet with the goal of resolving their differences.

Everyone hopes and prays that this is the end of the dispute, which has badly divided the Zappa fan base.

So what has happened to the best band you never heard in your life since they helped tell *Zappa The Hard Way's* story?

In 2013, Robert Martin (keyboards, vocals) became the musical director of the reformed Banned From Utopia ('A Tribute to the Music of Frank Zappa'), that has toured Europe in a variety of incarnations that have included Morgan Ågren (drums), Ed Mann (percussion), Chad Wackerman (drums), Ray White and Albert Wing (tenor saxophone).

At the end of 2016, I started a new interview with Wing (for my book, *Frank Talk: The Inside Stories of Zappa's Other People)*. After several exchanges, his emails suddenly stopped. I then learned why: he had suffered a stroke on February 1st, 2017 that disabled the motor functions on the right side of his body from head to foot.

In 2018, I asked him if he was now ready to reveal *"a hilarious little vignette, post-88"* that he had referred to in *Zappa The Hard Way*. He told me that *"I cannot remember the simple things since the stroke, and yet remember the ever so complicated: Frank's music. If and when it comes back, I will let you know."*

Bruce Fowler (trombone) too suffered a stroke that left him unable to play his instrument. His career as a composer, arranger, orchestrator and conductor of movie soundtracks continues apace, however.

Walt Fowler (trumpet) has toured and recorded with singer-songwriter

James Taylor (sometimes with Chad Wackerman) and Steve Gadd's band. And, like brother Bruce, he has helped orchestrate a number of blockbuster film soundtracks.

Paul Carman (alto saxophone) is currently with the improvisational band Forbits, who released the album *Jazz?* in 2015.

Ike Willis (guitar, vocals) continues to perform Frank's music with a variety of cover bands around the world.

As well as producing many more fine solo albums, Mike Keneally (guitar, keyboards, vocals) has toured and recorded with instrumental rock guitarist Joe Satriani.

In May 2017, Scott Thunes (bass) left the San Francisco Bay Area rock band Mother Hips, and was appointed 'ScoreMeister' (curator of Zappa's written music) by the ZFT.

Thunes, Keneally, Mann and Martin are now set to tour together again as part of the 'house band' that will perform with a hologram of Frank on "The Bizarre World Of Frank Zappa" tour in 2019.

While Frank Zappa (guitar, vocals) and Kurt McGettrick (baritone saxophone) left the building never to return, perhaps the most significant development for me since *Zappa The Hard Way* came about as a result of a conversation I had with Chad Wackerman back in 2010. I asked various band members if they had any photos from the tour that we could use in the book. Chad told me he hadn't but that, *"Frank hired a photographer named Sergio Albonico. I think he moved back to Italy. He may be a resource, as Frank hired him to take the programme photos."* I tried to get in touch with Sergio, but failed miserably at that time. I finally tracked him down last year (he has gone by the name of Milo since 1998) and my interview with him about the tour can be found in this book – along with many of his previously unseen photographs from band rehearsals, which form the centrepiece of this tome.

As well as Milo's photos, there are also a number of 'fan' shots included. By far the biggest contribution comes from Danish school teacher and hard-core fan, Ole Lysgaard. Ole got to know Frank well over the years, and he told me that *"whenever I went to a Frank concert I always brought with me a 'photographer' to take pictures so I could concentrate on the conversation with whoever I was talking with. In 1988, it was my friend Erling Agergaard, who did an excellent job. The colour concert photographs are from Copenhagen, and the black and white on stage shots from Würzburg. The photos of the various band members are all from Bremen, where I went with Bruce Fowler to a bar. The photo of him and myself is kind of fake because I do not drink beer or other alcoholic drinks at all. Yes, that is me thirty years ago, when my beard and hair had a completely different colour than it has now!"*

Also included in the book is the complete interview Frank's former secretary Pauline Butcher conducted with him after the first UK date of the 'Broadway' tour. Pauline kindly wrote the Afterword for the paperback version of *Zappa The Hard Way* in which she states, *"When I met him midway through the tour, Frank looked tired and drawn. It was sixteen years since I'd stopped working for him in Hollywood — an astonishing four-year period which I detail in my book, Freak Out! My Life With Frank Zappa. A few fleeting visits in between had reignited our bond. But in London in 1988, the whole afternoon stretched before us. Always polite and respectful, he answered my questions with honesty — even when I quizzed him about his sex life..."*

With my mission to document Frank Zappa's annus horribilis seemingly complete, let's bring the Republican Party up to date… well, in fact, Frank kind of did just that in 1989: pondering the state of the nation, he cited today's Republican President; with amazing prescience, he told Elin Wilder of High Times, *"Donald Trump is the idol of American teens — and teens can't read, write, or do arithmetic!"*

Who said facts are stupid things? **– Andrew Greenaway, March 2019**

[i] Post at The Official Frank Zappa Messageboards, July 2008.
[ii] Interview with Matt Resnicoff, Musician magazine, November 1991.
[iii] Zappa Family Trust press release, July 2015.
[iv] Interview with A.D. Amorosi, Magnet magazine, November 2016.

About The Author

Andrew Greenaway was born in Orpington, Kent, in 1958. He edits the UK's only Frank Zappa website (www.idiotbastard.com) and has curated several Zappa-themed albums for Cordelia Records. As well as writing *Zappa The Hard Way* (2010), *The Beatles... The Easy Way* (2014) and *Frank Talk: The Inside Stories Of Zappa's Other People* (2017) for Wymer UK, Andrew has contributed to *1001 Songs You Must Hear Before You Die* (Octopus Books, 2010), *We Are The Other People – 25 Years Of Zappanale* (Wehrhahn Verlag, 2014), *The Greatest Albums You'll Never Hear* (Octopus Books, 2014) and *The Zappa Tour Atlas* (Wymer UK, 2019). He also helped 'ghost' former football club owner Anton Johnson's memoir, *King Of Clubs* (Grosvenor House, 2012).

Andrew was one of the key contributors to *ZappaCast - The Frank Zappa Podcast* (www.zappa.com/zappacast) and now co-hosts *Andrew & Lee's Music Emporium* on SoundCloud. He also co-organises *Festival MOO-AH!*, a biennial celebration of Zappa's music in Corby, and is an auxiliary member of the Zappa Early Renaissance Orchestra.

Andrew has three children, two cats, one wife, and lives with them near the Thames Delta in darkest Essex. Aside from his family and music, his other interests include the Marx Brothers, Woody Allen, Kurt Vonnegut, Chelsea FC, Speedway GP, Coronation Street and having a right laugh.

About The Photographer

Milo Albonico is a photographer and painter, born in New York about 50 years ago.

In his spare time, he enjoys going alone to some big empty cinema so he can eat junk food and fall asleep in the middle of the film.

He loves animals, especially birds and cats.

He now lives in Nice, France.

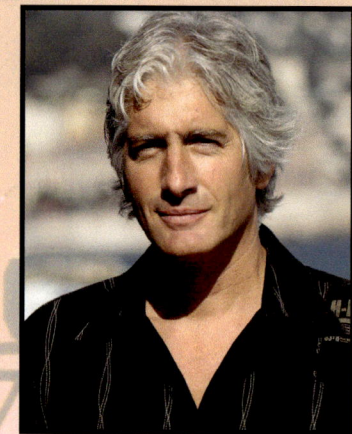

Cast of Tour Narrators

Morgan Ågren Guest drummer (with his partner, Mats Öberg)
Sergio "Milo" Albonico Official photographer
Lorraine Belcher Buxom red-haired companion
Pauline Butcher Secretary (1968 To 1972)
Paul Carman Alto saxophone
Warren Cuccurullo Guitar (February to April 1979)
Bruce Fowler Trombone
Walt Fowler Trumpet
Mike Keneally Stunt guitar/keyboards/vocals
Ed Mann Percussion
Robert "Bobby" Martin Keyboards/vocals
Kurt McGettrick Baritone saxophone
Mark Pinske Engineer (1979 to 1987)
Bob Rice Computer assistant/roadie
Merl Saunders Jr. Guitar tech
Scott Thunes Bass/Clonemeister
Fabio Treves Guest harmonicist
Chad Wackerman Drums
Ike Willis Guitar/vocals
Albert Wing Tenor saxophone
Dweezil Zappa Guest guitarist
Frank Zappa Guitar/vocals

Unless otherwise stated, all photos were taken by Milo Albonico and all quotes are taken from interviews conducted by the author.

BROADWAY THE HARD WAY
FRANK ZAPPA
BAND DRESSING ROOM

"Frank called me to say he wanted me in his new band that he was putting together. He said he had Mark (Volman) and Howard (Kaylan), and a new guy who played keyboards and guitar. I told him about my situation with Duran Duran: that I'd be joining as a full member, and I couldn't make myself available." —
Warren Cuccurullo

"During rehearsals, Ike was often late. But Frank accepted the situation because he needed a black singer and nobody could replace Ike. Frank would not say anything about Ike being late or not showing up at all sometimes." — Sergio Albonico

"Things started getting really tense between Scott and Chad, so Frank tried to split things up: for the last month of rehearsals, I was conducting the band and Scott was handling the dots on the page. My other job was to sit on Scott and make sure nobody killed him!" —
Ike Willis

"Originally it wasn't a tour: it was gonna be The Frank Zappa TV Show on Fox, and we were the house band. We'd rehearsed for a month and a half when Fox pulled the plug. So Frank felt it might make sense to do a tour." — Chad Wackerman
(from ZappaCast, Episode #50)

"His last tour, with some of the greatest musicians I've ever known, was my first. What a time that was." — Bob Rice
(from Facebook post on the 25th anniversary of Frank's passing, 2018)

"That was the finest band that I was involved in with Frank. It was the band we had been dreaming of. I lobbied to get the Fowler brothers back in the band. It was an incredible band and we had the right combination of people." — *Ike Willis* (from an interview with A.J. Abrams, March, 2000)

"There were a few hand signals that I never learnt — especially on the 1988 tour. I just couldn't remember them for some reason. We memorised a lot of music, over a hundred tunes. The horns were in rehearsal for two and a half months, eight hours a day, five days a week." — **Bruce Fowler** (from an interview with the Evil Prince, 1996)

"We had 120 tunes rehearsed, so it was completely different every night. Frank would change styles constantly. People might know a tune as reggae, but he might decide to do it as heavy metal. We rehearsed so much that Frank could change anything and the band could do it with confidence." —
Chad Wackerman (from an interview with Mitch Myers, January 2004)

"We rehearsed a lot of stuff. I don't remember any tunes that were thrown out — except for Forty-Four and Times Beach... he asked us if those tunes were playable, or should the computer play them?"
— **Walt Fowler**

"During King Kong Frank made me play guitar and keyboards simultaneously while singing at the same time, and also had me recite the 'headband' speech from Teen-age Wind which I doubled on guitar. Stairway ended with me on my knees at the front of the stage — all in all a heady experience for my first show with Frank." – **Mike Keneally**
(from Mike's Zappa Tour Diaries)

"There was the guys-who-loved-to-hang-out-with-Frank bus, and there was the salty old veterans' bus." — **Ike Willis**

"I got the whole back lounge to myself, virtually every night. On the other bus was everybody else in the band, and every night, all night long, Ike Willis would just be up and down the aisle, talking, talking, talking, just driving everybody bananas." — **Scott Thunes**

"Ike and Ed were both sleeping. It was a nice bus ride. Uncharacteristically quiet, because Ike was sleeping… I'm thinking that I may be switching to the other bus, because when Ike is awake there's no rest to be had." — **Mike Keneally**
(from Mike's Zappa Tour Diaries)

"The loss of manager Bennett Glotzer was a big one; Bennett made sure the family feeling was always present. The new, faceless managers were slick suit-wearing Hollywood hot-shots. Their approach was that Frank was walled off and isolated. The band and Frank were kept apart for much of the tour." — **Ed Mann**

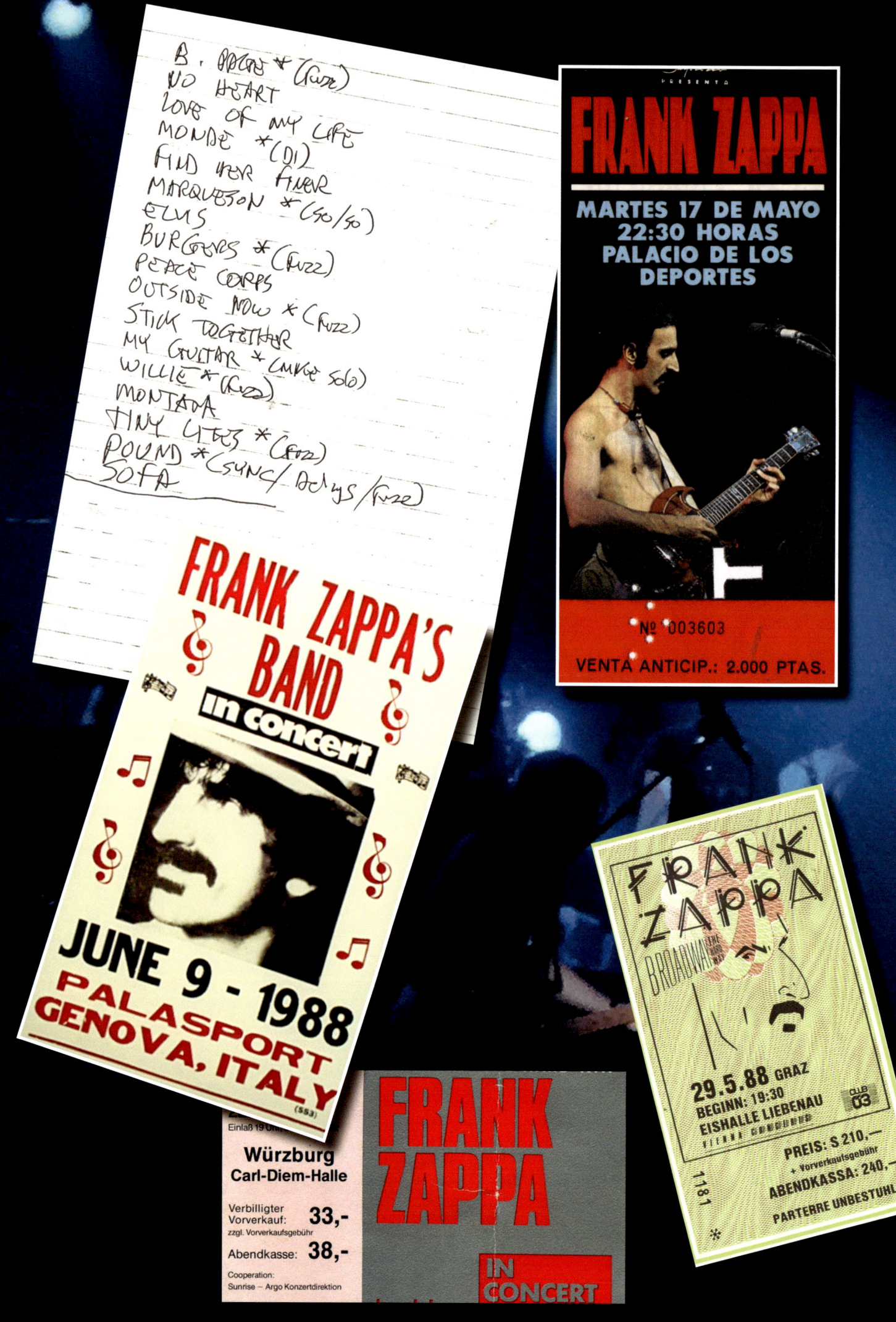

"I think most guitarists have a tendency to play like they talk in some way. And since I'm not much of a squealer — I happen to be a baritone kind of guy — to play on the low strings is a little more 'in phase with my reality.'" —
Frank Zappa
(from an interview with Alan di Perna, September 1988)

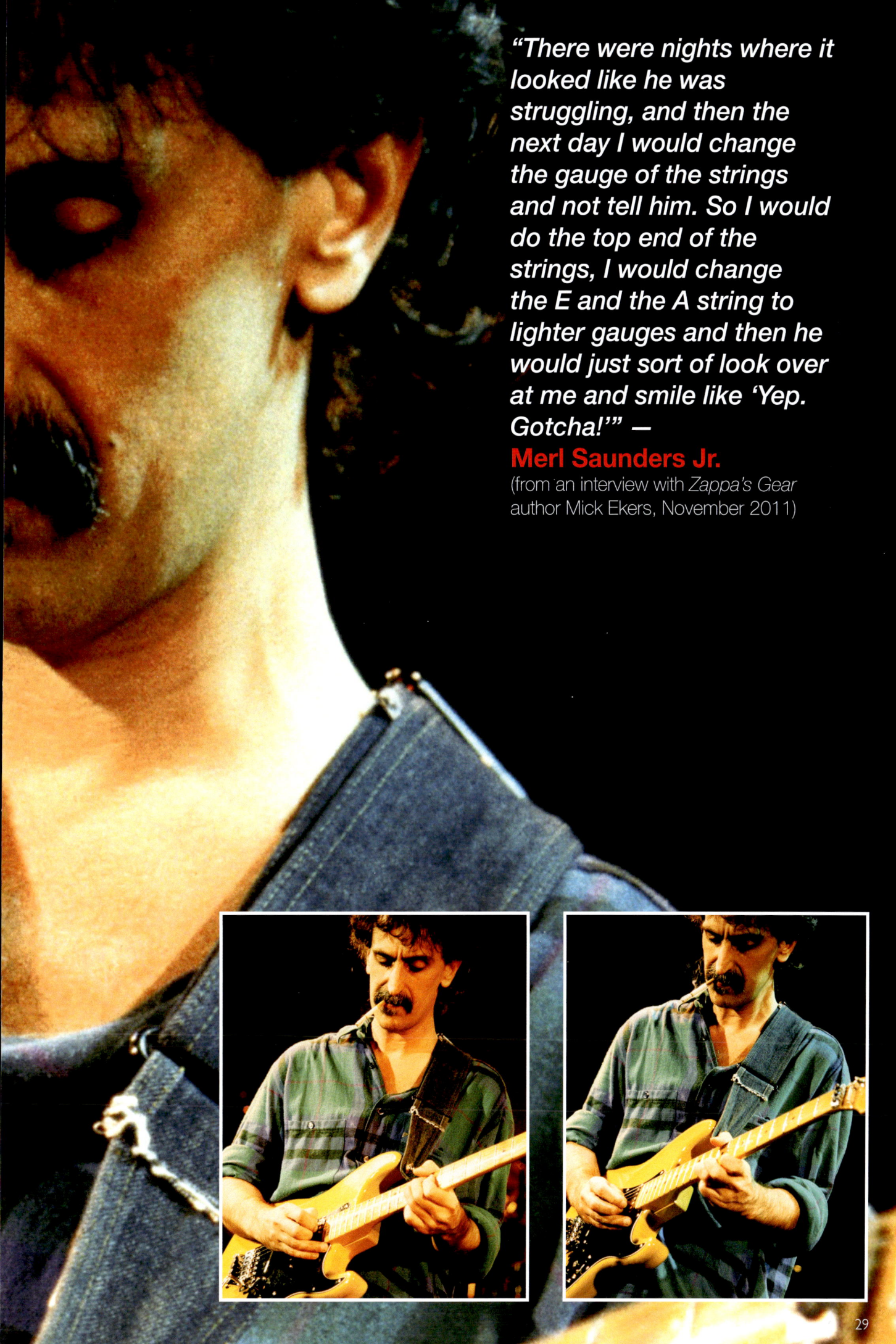

"There were nights where it looked like he was struggling, and then the next day I would change the gauge of the strings and not tell him. So I would do the top end of the strings, I would change the E and the A string to lighter gauges and then he would just sort of look over at me and smile like 'Yep. Gotcha!'" — **Merl Saunders Jr.**
(from an interview with *Zappa's Gear* author Mick Ekers, November 2011)

"He was amazing in the early seventies, but I couldn't hear him in 1988. It wasn't the PA, but... mentally. I remember Thunes coming up and saying, 'That solo was incredible,' but I was thinking, 'Jeez, I don't even remember it'. It's possibly my fault." –
Bruce Fowler
(from an interview with the Evil Prince, 1996)

(Photo Credit: Erling Agergaard from Ole Lysgaard's Collection)

"Dweezil plays heavy metal and he has a contract with Chrysalis. His new album is called My Guitar Wants to Kill Your Mama. He's eighteen." — **Frank Zappa** (from an interview with Pauline Butcher, April 1988)

The thing about that sound is, he's not playing through anything particularly special there. On that tour he was using a Roland GP8 that I programmed a bunch of sounds on, and that was like a $200 thing back in the 80s. But his guitar was set up very differently to a normal guitar so he was able to achieve that sound without a ton of extra hiss and noise. So it sounds good!"
— **Dweezil Zappa**
(from Peter Hodgson's I Heart Guitar blog, May 2012)

Milo and Frank, in Zappa's video vault on Woodrow Wilson Drive in the Hollywood Hills

INTERVIEW WITH 1988 TOUR PHOTOGRAPHER,
MILO ALBONICO
(aka SERGIO ALBONICO)

When I was writing *Zappa The Hard Way,* I tried to get in touch with Sergio Albonico. Sergio took the cover shots used on Frank's 1988 *Guitar* album, as well as all of the photos used in the 1988 tour's official programme. Principally I wanted to ascertain whether he had any outtakes we might include in the book, but I also thought he might have some interesting insights into the tour given that he attended many band rehearsals.

Alas, I was unable to trace him.

Fast forward nine years, and a Facebook friend contacted me having spotted some comments made by Sergio on a YouTube video. He seemed eager to tell some stories, so I made contact with him and conducted a very interesting and wide-ranging interview covering the tour, his time with jazz trumpeter Miles Davis, his relationship with Gail Zappa, friendships with electric bass player Jaco Pastorius and sexploitation film director Russ Meyer, and his career in the porn industry. That interview appears on my website at http://www.idiotbastard.com/Interviews/SergioAlbonico.htm.

In this follow-up interview, we talked more specifically about Frank and the 'Broadway The Hard Way' tour.

Tell me how you came to be at rehearsals for Frank Zappa's 1988 world tour.
I was living and working in Los Angeles in 1987. My next-door neighbour happened to be Bob Rice, who at the time was Zappa's Synclavier programmer. We became friends because we were both very passionate about music. I had been working as a photographer for music publications for two years and Bob liked my portraits of Miles Davis and his band, and he invited me to the rehearsals of Frank's upcoming tour. Zappa's band was rehearsing every day in a huge rented Hollywood sound stage which was previously part of the legendary Zoetrope Studios owned by Coppola.[i]

The first day I was at rehearsals I just watched all these great musicians that I knew from listening to them on records when I was younger, and then I felt that there were some great images to be captured, so I asked if I could take a few photos. A couple of days later, during rehearsals, Frank came up to me and asked me to show him what I had photographed so far. After having looked at some of my photos, he asked me in a very straightforward manner, *"How much do you want to make the tour book?"*

That's how I started to work with Frank.

So you were you familiar with Frank's music prior to that time?
Yes, I started listening to his music when I was sixteen. And the first album I heard of his remains my favourite to this day: *Zappa In New York*.[ii] This record perfectly captures what Zappa's music is all about.

I was also very familiar with the Warner Brothers' trilogy of *Studio Tan*,[iii] *Sleep Dirt*[iv] and *Orchestral Favorites*,[v] because a very dear friend of mine, Gary Panter, had done the artwork of these albums.[vi]

Also, I can play the piano and read music so I knew damn well how intricate Frank's music can be… it can go from a one chord blues line to suddenly a complicated classically arranged composition, and then dive into extremely controlled guitar solos…and everything has to be perfect. Mistakes were not allowed. Not so many musicians can handle the level of perfection that Frank demanded with his music.

Of course, there were many musicians there who had played with Frank before, but there was also the new guy, Mike Keneally. Mike talked about being confused as to whether Ike Willis was in the band or not at the outset. Was it clear to you?
If there was one musician who, in Frank's vision, was impossible to replace it was Ike Willis. Ike represented something very important for Frank.

Ike Willis was Frank's alter ego in music. Frank absolutely needed this element. Ike was like a 'mirror image' for Frank: a singer he loved to sing with.

Ike was Joe,[vii] and Joe was Frank.

I understand Mike's confusion about Ike Willis… Ike was skipping rehearsals sometimes, and the band could not rehearse the tunes where he was singing. Frank didn't like that but he knew he had to accept it. There was absolutely no question about Ike being replaced.

During rehearsals, I saw some auditions for drummers at one point, that's all. One time I also saw Bruce Bickford,[viii] the clay animator. Frank had invested a lot of money on his work.

Mike Keneally was the 'new guy', a very nice gentleman indeed. He had learned all Zappa's music by himself. He was so happy to be in Frank's band. He was so relaxed and attentive to everything that was happening.

What did you think of the horn section — something Frank hadn't really used for a number of years?
The horn section was what made all the difference on this tour.

A five-piece horn section: baritone, tenor sax and alto sax, trombone and trumpet. The horn section is ever present on all the compositions played on the 1988 tour.

The Fowler brothers had played with Frank since the seventies. The other guys were all top session players, probably recommended by Bruce Fowler.

I must say that all the musicians in Frank's band were very educated people in all areas, not just music. And the same I can say about Miles Davis' musicians.

Frank's horn section shines in so many situations. I remember how great it sounded in tunes like *Black Napkins* and *Big Swifty*. Albert Wing was probably the more eclectic player and soloist of the horn section.

On the wonderful images you captured, Mike and everyone else look happy to be there. Did you see any signs of discontent then?
Thank you for the compliment! Most of these photos have not been seen nor published before.

I don't remember any discontent. It was work. Putting together a band like that takes a lot of energy and patience. Mainly because they were

all musicians with their own specific personality and the music had to be perfect.

Zappa's band was formed around a basic group of musicians Frank had been working with for quite a few years: Frank, Ike Willis, Ed Mann, Scott Thunes, Chad Wackerman and Bobby Martin.

The new guys were Mike Keneally, Paul Carman, Kurt McGettrick and Albert Wing.

The 'old' guys were Bruce Fowler and Walt Fowler.

The person responsible for the horn section and the horn section's musical arrangements was Bruce Fowler.

Frank had decided that when he was not present, it was Scott Thunes' responsibility to conduct the whole band during rehearsals.

Scott is a great guy, a lot of fun to be with. He was very friendly to me. After rehearsals one time he took me to a 'death rock' club. He liked that type of atmosphere.

Scott was also a comedian on stage while he was playing very difficult parts on the bass. He had a cynical kind of humour and not everybody understood his behaviour.

I remember that while I was photographing the band, he would kick my rolls of film that I had left beside my photo bag, or he would hide my equipment. I didn't take it personally at all. I thought it was funny, but I noticed that he was under some kind of stress. I found out later that his brother had recently passed away.[ix]

But I believe that the confusion started when he was arguing with the horn section and then Chad started having problems playing when Scott was conducting.

Scott was a little bit of a prankster. Not everybody appreciated his behaviour. He was probably not the best choice for conducting the band.

Along with Ike, Bobby and Ed, Scott was a great comedian on stage as well — just like Patrick O'Hearn[x] before.

Do you think Frank was aware of the issues between Scott and the horn section? Ike describes a time during rehearsals when he had to tell everyone to go to lunch to calm down - he said his job was to sit on Scott and make sure nobody killed him when Frank wasn't around.
Scott was playing an electric wireless bass. So he was one of the few musicians in the group who could walk anywhere he wanted and still play.

The band was rehearsing in this huge soundstage. The UMRK[xi] recording truck with Bob Stone[xii] inside the truck was also inside the soundstage.

With his wireless bass, Scott could not stay still all the time. I remember more than once we could all hear Scott playing but nobody knew where he was…he was hiding somewhere, but still playing complicated bass patterns of tunes — *Alien Orifice*, probably. Frank had nominated him bandleader.

When he would come out of hiding, he would sometimes argue with some musician: didn't really matter who.

I think Frank was not aware of the issues. I think something happened with Chad and Scott at one point. I don't remember well because I had other things to think about on my end. Maybe it was between Ed and Scott. But at one point, Scott had the whole band upset with him. I don't know exactly why.

Scott himself is unsure why too. It always struck me as odd that after playing together for so many years, Scott and Chad – this solid rhythm section — should fall out. Scott told me he didn't even speak with Chad once they got out on the road.
Chad is also a friend of mine. One time I remember we went out with jazz saxophonist Wayne Shorter to listen to live Brazilian music in a club in LA. We had a great time. When in Wayne's company, there is always peace and joy around.

Chad is one of the very few drummers who can play Zappa's music. And he's fun to be around. Chad's drum set was full of electronic devices everywhere.

I think the problem lies in Zappa's decision to have Scott as bandleader when he was absent. Probably Bobby Martin would have been a better bandleader. But maybe Bobby didn't want to do that.

As well as the tour book, your photos were also used for Frank's *Guitar* album. Tell me about the selection of the shots used.
Frank explained to me that he wanted a red photo portrait of himself for the double album that he was going to title simply, *Guitar*. Frank told me that the album cover had to be red because the colour red is commercial.

So I started using different kinds of film to get different types of red.

Then I did my first selection and gave a lot of photos to Frank to look at.

I don't know who made the final choices for the album cover, but I am pretty sure it was Frank's wife Gail.

Was Gail ever around during rehearsals?
Gail was never around. She only came on the last night of rehearsals with her sons, Dweezil and Ahmet.

I am sorry to say this, but I know some of the musicians in the band didn't appreciate her presence.

My personal working experience with Gail was not good. She was... how can I say… aggressive.

I know that both Gail and Frank liked Scott — which may not have helped the situation. But why do you think Frank didn't intervene and resolve the difficulties once they became readily apparent on the tour?
Could it be because at the time Scott was also playing from time to time with a young Dweezil Zappa?

Well, so was Chad Wackerman: he and Scott were the rhythm section on his 1986 debut album, *Havin' A Bad Day,* produced by Frank.

I assume all of the photos used in the tour book were taken during rehearsals – did you see any dates on the tour?
All the photos used in the tour book were taken during rehearsals. I saw only one date of the tour, and that's when I also found out that the band was having a hard time on the tour. I found out that basically nobody was talking to Scott.

I then continued to work in the music business and I started producing a couple of jazz albums for PolyGram/Verve Forecast. I hired Mike Stern,[xiii] Bob Berg,[xiv] Wayne Shorter, Allan Holdsworth[xv] and John Patitucci[xvi] as session players. This lead to another project where I hired Miles Davis for a recording session for a song of a movie soundtrack,[xvii] and so I started to work with Miles — which lead to producing a song on a Santana album.[xviii] So I saw different music situations.

Did you ever discuss Frank's music with Miles?
I never discussed Frank's music with Miles. I don't believe I was in a position to do that.

I did an interview with Miles for Keyboard magazine: this is mentioned in a book titled *Miles On Miles*.[xix]

I think that at the time, Miles' and Frank's bands were legendary because they both were music geniuses who would regularly hire young musicians who would later become worldwide superstars.

When talking to Miles, I was always intimidated by his aura.

How did you feel about Frank — did you find him intimidating at all?
Frank was a very kind man. He was very kind to me.

During the time I worked with him, I knew I was working with a living legend.

My job was to capture Frank and the band in the most natural way. I preferred not to speak to Frank so much because he was always one step ahead of everyone else. It was more interesting and logical for me to capture moments that you cannot plan — they just happen.

Did I find Frank intimidating? I can't say. I was working with Miles and Frank at the same time. I just didn't want to get in the way of their work.

I was very happy to be accepted by this unique... army of musicians. I became friends with Scott, Ed and Chad, and that was great.

I must say that the few times I saw Frank really happy and smiling it was definitely when he was with Ike Willis. Ike always made him smile. He had that power!

One of my favourite songs on *Make A Jazz Noise Here* is *Advance Romance*. Listening to that song brings me a lot of memories. It's a song where there is a lot of interaction between singers and crazy stuff happens. Only Zappa or Miles can pull off music like that, in my humble opinion.

The only other band I can think of at that level is George Duke's band with Napoleon Murphy Brock,[xx] Sheila E[xxi] and Leon 'Ndugu' Chancler[xxii] in 1978. Never a dull moment!

We all know Frank is the first rock musician who experimented and succeeded in blending crazy funny lyrics and stories with sophisticated avant-garde classical music and blues. And we have to be thankful for that.

Imagine a world where *Lumpy Gravy*[xxiii] never happened. It's a scary thought.

In interviews Frank said he liked Miles' music, and Miles' must've at least been aware of Frank's – he worked with George Duke[xxiv] and, didn't you tell me, he wanted Terry Bozzio[xxv] in his band at one point?
Frank would incorporate different styles of music in his compositions, including jazz and blues.

That's why George Duke was so important when he was in Frank's Mothers Of Invention: he contributed so much, and on quite a few albums. Black musicians who worked with Zappa always brought to his music the 'warm' human element.

I did a few photo sessions for Remo drums and Paiste cymbals with Terry Bozzio. Yes, Miles wanted Terry to play in his band. At the time Terry's Missing Persons[xxvi] was very popular and all the members of this group had incredible haircuts and costumes. Miles loved Terry's fashion style and he did ask him to play in this band to replace Al Foster.

Musicians in Miles' band would call Miles 'The Chief'. The Chief wanted a rock drummer exactly like Terry, because he sounded great and looked incredible on stage.

As a young drummer, Terry had already transcribed and learned many Tony Williams'[xxvii] drum solos and jazz patterns. Tony Williams is Terry's number one favourite drummer.

But Terry turned down Miles because he didn't feel comfortable about it. He turned down Bowie as well. He wanted to move on with his solo career and be a pop singer and composer. This all lead to Terry finally forming with Jeff Beck the super trio of *Guitar Shop*.[xxviii]

It would have been amazing to see and hear Terry playing with Miles. But I think that he surely would have had to endure a lot of pressure when on the road with the band.

Miles could be quite cynical at times, saying things like, *"Music has no friends..."* Or saying that white musicians play behind the beat or too loud. He was probably right.

And Terry was definitely a wonderful choice. It would have been Miles' first and only white drummer playing with him. Miles as a band conductor wanted always to be very close to the drummer to get new ideas, as we all know. And Terry is one of the most eclectic drummers who are also concerned about stage presentation and showmanship, something that Miles was very hungry for.

In spite of the problems, would you agree that the music Frank's 1988 band produced was mostly fantastic?
The 1988 band was the biggest line-up Frank ever had…

Well, at least since the 20-piece Grand Wazoo line-up in 1972.
I didn't know that!

But it was similar to the same line-up of the double album *Zappa In New York*. Only that in 1988 there was a new set of amazing musicians and personalities, just like in 1976 with *In New York*.

It was wonderful to witness the evolution of this band and capture the energy of all the musicians involved.

The band rehearsed every day for a period of over three months. Rehearsals started at five in the afternoon.

Usually around 9pm, Frank would arrive at rehearsals. Frank did not have a driver's licence. It was his choice; he didn't want to drive ever. Just like Quincy Jones. There are people who cannot handle driving (like me, as well).

The band would work on the music until about two or three in the morning.

Frank had the habit of sleeping during the day and working at night.

What made this band unique is that all the musicians were also great human beings. I remember them all very dearly. And of course there was the Synclavier,[xxix] which added some amazing amplified sound effects – burps, snorks and other surround sound noises, all created by Frank (with help from Bob Rice). The Synclavier was one of Frank's favourite instruments.[xxx] Eddie Jobson's too.

What we can listen to today are the live albums — *Make A Jazz Noise Here, Broadway The Hard Way* and *The Best Band You Never Heard In Your Life* — which document only part of the music that Frank's band

played on the road.

It was a band that for the first time featured an ever-present five-piece horn section.

I personally have fond memories of tunes such as *Big Swifty, Strictly Genteel, Black Napkins, Inca Roads, Cosmik Debris* and *The Black Page*.

Re-listening to the two double albums, I noticed that the mix volume of the singers is a bit low — we don't hear Ike and Bobby very well. Bobby Martin was incredible when he would sing *Whippin' Post* or *The Illinois Enema Bandit* — songs which, unfortunately, didn't make it onto any of those live albums.

Yes, so here's hoping more from 1988 will be released from the Zappa Vault in the not too distant future.

Frank would often use hand signals for the band to change tempo or play in a particular style. Did you see him rehearse any of these with the band?

The hand signals were called 'hand cues'. Frank had developed many hand cues by then — the most frequent was the reggae cue — just short five, or even three, second cues. There was one where Frank would twist his hand and the entire band would do the same with their instrument.

There was also one where Frank would smoke a cigarette and sit down to listen to the band and hear them express themselves, and one for Chad to play hard free rock, and Frank would pick his guitar and improvise.

Let's take the song *Big Swifty* from the *Make A Jazz Noise Here* album. For the first 37 seconds, the band plays the theme. Then at 00:37, Frank gives the cue to go into a short brass section statement that ends at 00:53, when Frank gives the cue to go into jazz. You can even hear Frank saying, *"Everybody…"*, and also at 1:15, when he says, *"Make a jazz noise here,"* and there is a short cue until 1:21 of just two seconds that opens the way to Bruce Fowler's trombone solo, which lasts until 2:55. Time for Frank to light up a cigarette and listen to the band.

At 2:55, Frank decides to take the band into a Bizet/Carmen arrangement and conducts the band with the stick. That lasts until 3:42, where Frank gives a cue to go into a brass section interlude. Then at 4:04, Frank gives a cue of only three seconds — so until 4:07 — where Frank gives the cue which leads directly into a super piano solo played by Bobby Martin. Bobby's solo lasts a little less than two minutes, in which time Frank can smoke another cigarette. And usually it's now that Scott would walk up to Frank to find out what was going to happen next.

At 6:12, the brass section comes back in… what's going to happen next? A burning sax solo at 6:51 begins with heavy swinging be-bop style phrasing, and the drumming stops suddenly at 8:07 for a short three second cue to then another resolutory cue to the Synclavier, operated by Bob Rice, which opens at 8:10 the jazz solo of Ed Mann's genial percussion and voices; Frank's Synclavier sounds, which were ominous burps and snorks and scary buzzes; and Chad's electric pads. This amazing solo lasts until 9:26 when Frank stops the Ed, Chad and Synclavier solo for 5 seconds… and we're back into the *Big Swifty* theme.

These were Zappa's cues — in a song of 11:12 — many, many hand cues.

He also had a cue for the band to play a Fake Devo texture[xxxii] — did you see him use that one?
Zappa was a Devo fan! In fact, he had a Devo cue where the singers in the band would immediately sing a cappella — a fast, single note repetition. If you listen to Zappa's song *Mother People*, there are some similarities with Devo's song *Jocko Homo*… the repetitions of the same note.

Bruce Fowler was also working on an arrangement of a Devo song called *Mongoloid* for Frank.

I think Frank liked the abstract but rigidly structured arrangements of Devo's songs and the hidden double meanings of Devo's lyrics mocking society's 'de-evolution', which was a subject very dear to him.

I was also working with Mark Mothersbaugh at the time (on an interview for Keyboard magazine in Japan), and so I invited Mark to see Zappa's rehearsal. At that time Mark, composer and lead singer of Devo, was just starting his career as a movie composer with his theme for the *Pee-wee's Playhouse*[xxxiii] show. I introduced him to Frank, who told him that he had just received an offer from Alejandro Jodorowsky[xxxiv] to compose the music of his upcoming film, *Santa Sangre*.[xxxv] Of course, it never happened. But Mark Mothersbaugh is to this day one of my very best friends and we still work together on projects.

Cool. You've talked about some of the guys in Frank's 1988 band — is there anyone else you'd like to mention?
Ed Mann I thought he was a genius. His was the most complex instrument set-up: vibes, xylophones – all kinds of unusual percussion, as well as laughing boxes and various toys. Let's not forget that the previous percussionist was Ruth Underwood.[xxxvi]

Ed was so much fun to be around. He had a great sense of humour and never skipped a beat.

His parts were extremely difficult, and he was just as irreplaceable as Ike Willis.

Ed was responsible for all the funny sounds that would sometimes interact with the Synclavier, guided by Frank. Ed had also just published a book for malletists.[xxxvii]

His assorted percussion and impeccable malletist artistry and technique enriched Frank's music with a unique and colourful sound.

Okay, final question: fans will be familiar with the name Sergio Albonico, from the *Guitar* album and 1988 tour programme. Why is it that these days you go by the name of Milo?
In 1990, to everyone in the world's concern, the Gulf War started.

I decided to take a work offer from Rome with an erotic film agency, Diva Futura, owned by Cicciolina.[xxxviii] I was the house photographer and, eventually, manager of the agency.

Later I was asked by a film distributor to make a series of porn films, which I was happy to accept because I was given a lot of freedom to film anything I wished to.

Knowing that I had to make at least twenty films – of one hour and thirty minutes each — in a short time, I came up with the solution of creating a series of films called *Pussy Heaven*. I also made the choice of treating this series like some kind of sex journal. Each film treated a different argument (like in those erotic German films from the early seventies, such as *Schulmädchen-Report)*,[xxxix] and I felt right away that I also had to be in

front of the camera telling the stories. It was a matter of integrity: I believed that if you are going to make a sex film you should have the courage to also be yourself in your own film having sex. So I did.

I decided to use my second name Milo to sign all the films that I was about to make, just like changing skin. It felt good and I was working with some incredible women. In my films, there are always a lot of women.

I had to deliver one film every month. I was filming mainly in the Czech Republic and Berlin.

Since 1998, people still call me Milo to this day.

Thanks for your time — and your photos — Milo!
Interview conducted on 3rd January 2019

[i] American film director and screenwriter, Francis Ford Coppola, responsible for films such as *The Godfather* (1972), *Apocalypse Now* (1979), *Rumble Fish* (1983) and *Bram Stoker's Dracula* (1992).
[ii] Originally released in 1977.
[iii] Released in 1978.
[iv] Released in 1979, and originally titled *Hot Rats III*.
[v] Released in 1978.
[vi] After Warner Brothers belatedly removed the track *Punky's Whips* from the *Zappa In New York* album, Zappa claimed breach of contract and sued them. In an attempt to fulfil his contractual obligations, he had sent the label the masters for three other albums. Without Zappa's knowledge, Warners hired Panter to provide the cover art for all three.
[vii] Lead character in Zappa's three-part rock opera, *Joe's Garage* (1979).
[viii] Provided claymation for Zappa's films *A Token Of His Extreme* (1976), *Baby Snakes* (1979), *The Dub Room Special!* (1982), *The Amazing Mr. Bickford* (1987) and *Video From Hell* (1987).
[ix] Thunes told the author that his brother, Derek *"got in a very bad motorcycle accident that eventually killed him"* around 1986, and also that his *"dad died in 1988"*, but stressed that he *"wasn't in any state of negativity about anything ever"* until the tour reached Springfield.
[x] Zappa's bass player from 1976 to 1978.
[xi] Utility Muffin Research Kitchen.
[xii] Zappa's recording engineer from 1980 to 1992, who sadly died in 2005.
[xiii] Grammy-nominated American jazz guitarist.
[xiv] American jazz saxophonist (1951–2002).
[xv] English guitarist and composer (1946-2017).
[xvi] American jazz bassist.
[xvii] *Capri* (1991), written by Italian film composer, Carlo Rustichelli.
[xviii] *Full Moon* on Santana's 1990 album, *Spirits Dancing In The Flesh* — which was co-produced by drummer Chester 'Cortez' Thompson, with songs arranged by Peter F. Wolf.
[xiv] On page 274 of the book *Miles On Miles: Interviews And Encounters With Miles Davis* (Lawrence Hill Books, 2008), edited by Paul Maher Jr. and Michael K. Dorr.
[xx] Zappa's singer/saxophonist from 1973 to 1984.
[xxi] American percussionist/singer, Sheila Escovedo.
[xxii] American pop, funk and jazz drummer (1952–2018).
[xxiii] Zappa's first solo album, released in 1968.
[xxiv] Zappa's keyboard player from 1970 to 1975.
[xxv] Zappa's drummer from 1975 to 1978.
[xxvi] Band founded in 1980 by Bozzio with guitarist Warren Cuccurullo and vocalist Dale Bozzio.
[xxvii] American jazz drummer (1945-1997).
[xxviii] The English rock guitarist's 1989 instrumental rock album, featuring Bozzio and keyboard player Tony Hymas.
[xxix] A digital synthesizer and sampler manufactured by New England Digital.
[xxx] In *The Real Frank Zappa Book*, Frank wrote, "the Synclavier allows the composer not only to have his piece performed with precision, but to style the performance as well — he can bring his idea to the audience in a pure form, allowing them to hear the music, rather than the ego problems of a group of players who don't give a shit about the composition. Machines don't get loaded, drunk or evicted and don't need assistance moving their families around in 'emergency' situations. On the other hand, machines don't decide to say things like 'We're Beatrice' in precisely the 'wrong' place in the middle of a song, and make people laugh (one of Ike Willis's specialties)."
[xxxi] Zappa's violinist/keyboard player from 1975 to 1976. His 1985 solo album, *Theme Of Secrets*, was a showcase for the Synclavier.
[xxxii] In *The Real Frank Zappa Book*, he described this as, "...anything absolutely squared off, mechanical, dry and dead-sounding. Invocation of this plasticized mantra adds another dimension to a lyric."
[xxxiii] American children's television programme, starring Paul Reubens as the childlike Pee-wee Herman, which ran from 1986 to 1990 on Saturday mornings.
[xxxiv] Chilean-French filmmaker.
[xxxv] *Santa Sangre (Holy Blood),* a 1989 Mexican-Italian avant-garde horror film, co-written, starring and directed by Jodorowsky.
[xxxvi] Zappa's percussionist from 1969 to 1976.
[xxxvii] *The Essential Mallet Player* (Monad Publishing, 1986), that gives *"modal, tonal, and technical concepts for beginning to advanced players of the vibraphone, marimba, xylophone and all other mallet keyboards"*.
[xxxvii] Hungarian-Italian porn star/politician/singer, Ilona Staller.
[xxxix] 1970 West German pseudo-documentary film directed by Ernst Hofbauer, released in the UK as *Confessions Of A Sixth Form Girl*.

"The stunt guitarist's role is to reproduce guitar parts I've done on old records, because I can't sing and play lead guitar at the same time onstage. This year's stunt guitar player is also a very excellent guy named Michael Keneally." — **Frank Zappa** (from an interview with Alan di Perna, September 1988)

"Ike is taken with my abilities and my attitude, and lack of ego when it comes to being told by Frank to play something. I just play it like I'm supposed to do. No big deal to me, but apparently other people have bridled at the idea of playing the parts which are dictated to them without immediately embellishing upon them. I'm more than happy to play the stuff as written." — **Mike Keneally** (from Mike's Zappa Tour Diaries)

(Photo Credit: Erling Agergaard from Ole Lysgaard's Collection)

"We just had so much fun. I'd be trying to do my job, and Frank would slide over and in the middle of a verse he'd say something, and I'm on the floor. Now I've got to get him back. And we could go on like that all night long. That was the hardest tour!" — **Ike Willis**

"We have several songs about Pat Robertson, but fortunately his Presidential campaign went nowhere, though he spent more money than all the rest of the guys. I think that it's a good indication that there's still a few sane people left in the United States." — **Frank Zappa**
(from an interview with Pauline Butcher, April 1988)

"We put that together in one afternoon. It's a mini oratorio. We did it because a lot of people already know those songs and it would be absurd to hear this band playing Norwegian Wood, Lucy In The Sky With Diamonds and Strawberry Fields. And that's how the thing got started; I said it would just surprise people if we did it. So we started working on it in rehearsal and I decided to re-write the words to those songs and make it all about Jimmy Swaggart." — **Frank Zappa** (from an interview with Kevin Matthews on WLUP Chicago, March 1988)

"My thoughts on 1988 are very few and quite scattered, not to mention mostly missing. But if you were to ask me now, after having read Zappa The Hard Way, I would say that Ed Mann might have had a good point if he were to answer that Frank was 'tired' and 'sick with butt-cancer' and that it was pure laziness that allowed him to add songs he didn't write." — **Scott Thunes**

"*I always liked Boléro, I think that it's really one of the best melodies ever written, and most people in the audience have heard it in one form or another over the years. So in conducting an experiment into arranging technique – this is a reggae version of the Boléro — it's nice to be arranging a tune that people are already familiar with.*" — **Frank Zappa**
(from an interview with Charles Amirkhanian, April 1991)

"Other groups that go out with horn sections, their basic function is to play the little punches and pads and boop-boop-boops in between what the electric instruments are doing. That's not a very gratifying life for a horn player to just play a few notes and spend the rest of the night banging on Latin percussion instruments. We don't do that." — Frank Zappa
(from The Real Frank Zappa Book by Frank Zappa with Peter Occhiogrosso)

"Scott, when we're playing lines together it'd be really great if you could come over to my side of the stage." —
Kurt McGettrick
(as quoted by Thunes in the book
*In Cold Sweat:
Interviews With Really Scary
Musicians* by Thomas Wictor)

"Yeah, Scott, we don't feel like you're playing behind us — we feel like you're just going off on some other tangents while we're playing." —
Paul Carman
(as quoted by Thunes in the book
*In Cold Sweat:
Interviews With Really Scary
Musicians* by Thomas Wictor)

"Scott, we're all in this together. We're all trying to do the right thing; we're all trying to have a good time here. Some people are a little bit harsher than others, and you're the harshest of them all. You know, I've never met anybody who's so caustic as you, and maybe you wanna think about that." — **Frank Zappa** (to Thunes, as quoted by him in the book In *Cold Sweat: Interviews With Really Scary Musicians* by Thomas Wictor)

"I tried to engage Sting in casual conversation; a full length mirror commanded his attention, which provided a more convivial atmosphere for him." —
Albert Wing

"*I invited Sting to the show. During intermission, he came backstage and I asked him if he wanted to come out and do something with us. First he said no and I said, 'There's no way that you can lose because this band will always make you look good,' and I gave him a yellow pad and a pen and I said, 'Just right out what you're gonna do and we'll do it: no rehearsal'. And he did it.*" – **Frank Zappa**
(from an interview with Kevin Matthews on WLUP Chicago, March 1988)

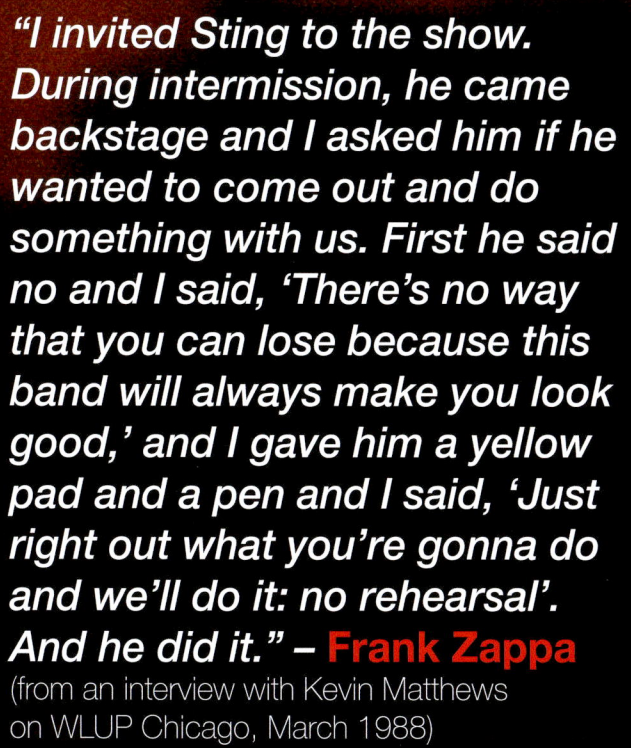

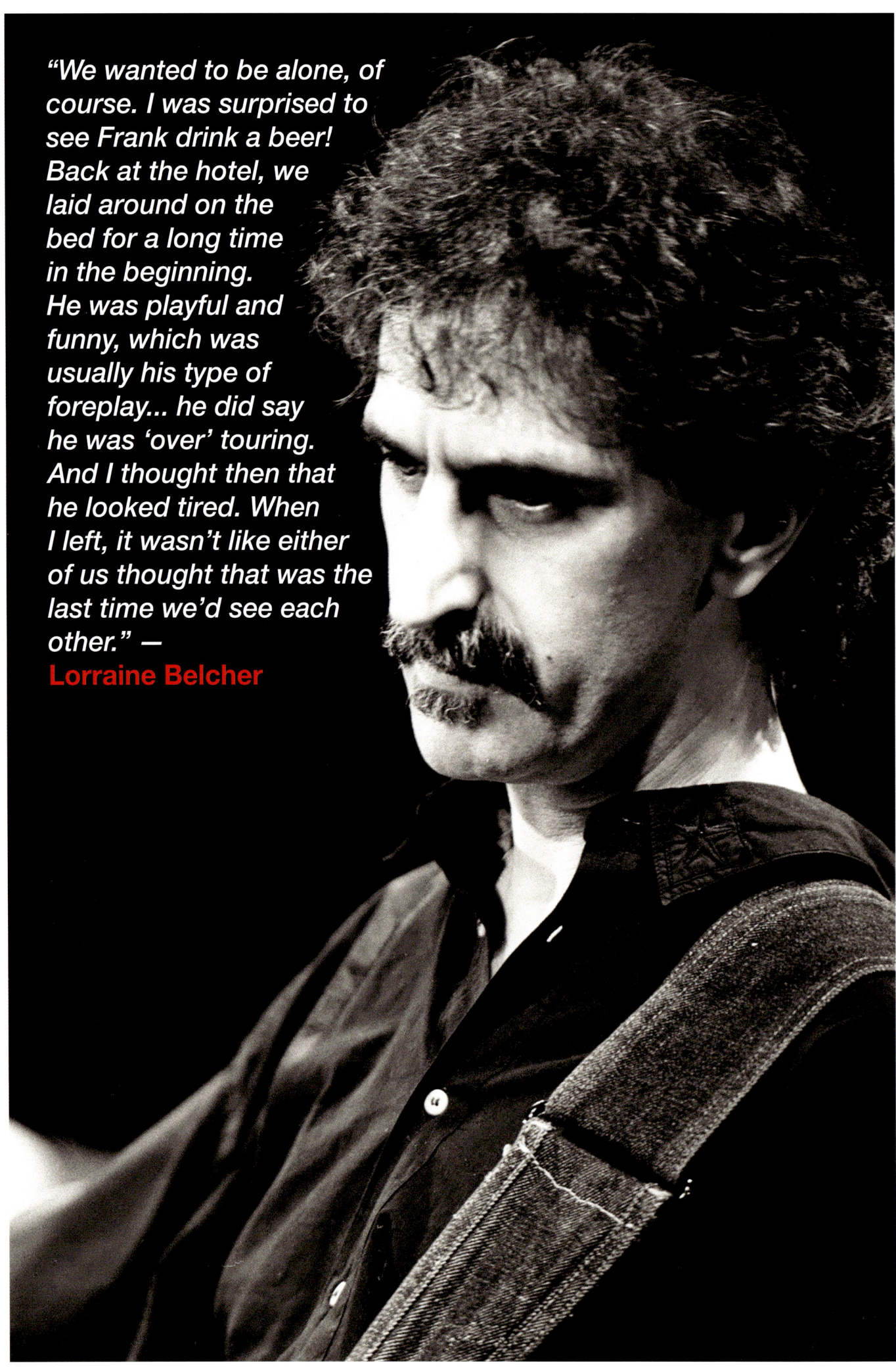

"We wanted to be alone, of course. I was surprised to see Frank drink a beer! Back at the hotel, we laid around on the bed for a long time in the beginning. He was playful and funny, which was usually his type of foreplay... he did say he was 'over' touring. And I thought then that he looked tired. When I left, it wasn't like either of us thought that was the last time we'd see each other." —
Lorraine Belcher

"Generally I agreed with Frank about politics. I thought he was a brilliant spokesman about freedom of speech. I could really get behind what he was talking about. I'm sure if we hadn't had the demise of the band, I'm sure that could have happened even more." — **Bruce Fowler** (from an interview with the Evil Prince, 1996)

"Here in the hotel, I don't have a piano. I tried to rent one, but it was too ungodly expensive. So I just sit and write it out and take it to the next soundcheck with the band and pass out the parts and play it right away." — **Frank Zappa**
(from an interview with Pauline Butcher, April 1988)

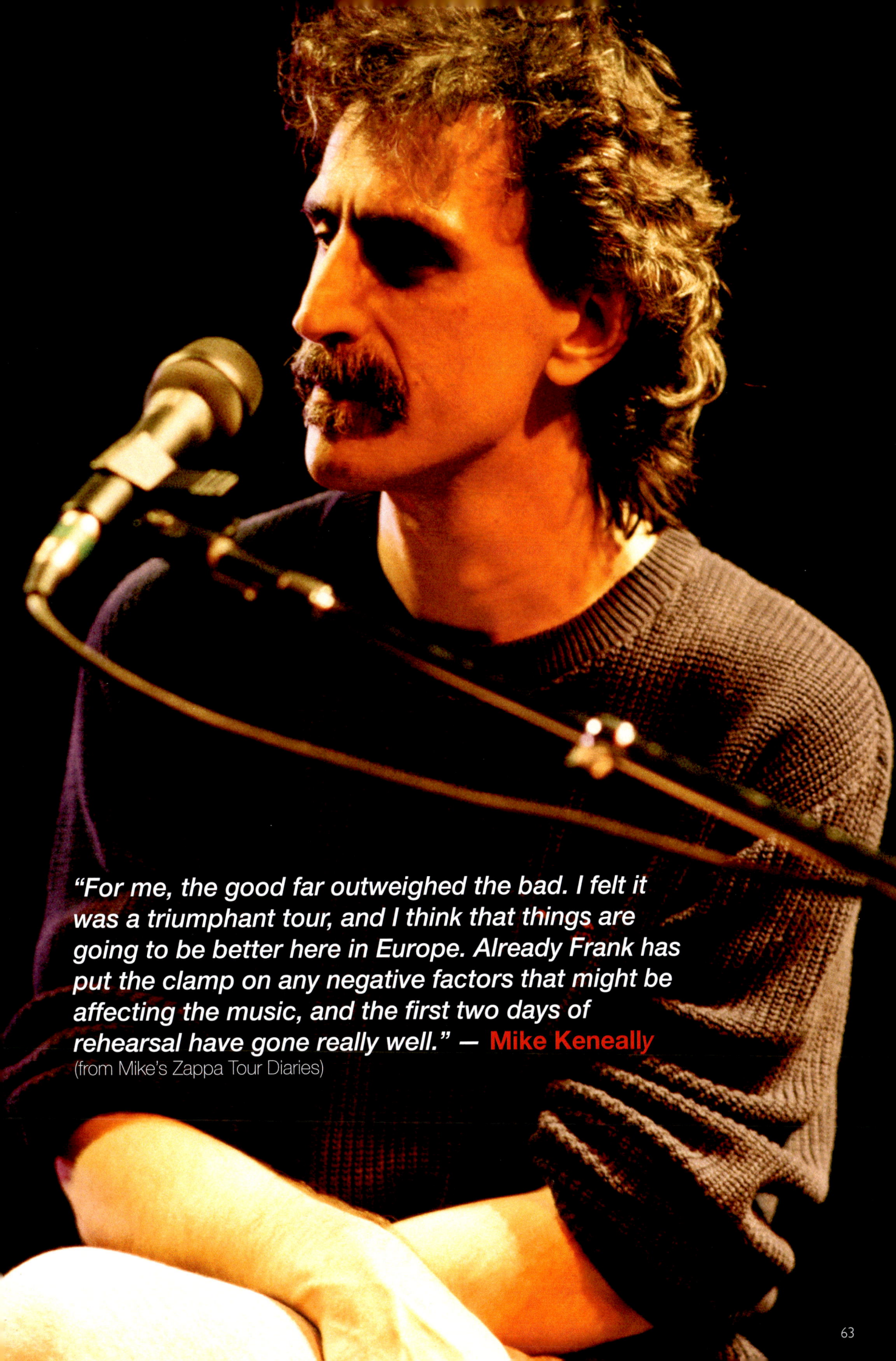

"For me, the good far outweighed the bad. I felt it was a triumphant tour, and I think that things are going to be better here in Europe. Already Frank has put the clamp on any negative factors that might be affecting the music, and the first two days of rehearsal have gone really well." — Mike Keneally
(from Mike's Zappa Tour Diaries)

"In the middle of the tour, I understood everybody's side, and I let Frank know that whatever happens, I'm on his side, totally. Because you wait that long to play with Frank, I just wanted to continue. I was just getting started on this gig and I was one of the new kids on the block. I just still had a lot of that energy." — **Albert Wing** (from an interview with Fred Banta, March 2000)

(Photo Credit: Erling Agergaard from Ole Lysgaard's Collection)

"At last night's concert in Brighton, the audience was skinheads, punks, weekend beachgoers - whoever those people are that go to Brighton for an amazing Saturday night experience. They were quite mixed, they were quite young, they were very drunk, and there was one guy who was pressed right up to the barricade in the front who was vomiting — which is a little tough to watch while you're singing."
— **Frank Zappa**
(from an interview with Pauline Butcher, April 1988)

FRANKLY SPEAKING

ROY WILKINSON grills FRANK ZAPPA

PAVEMENTING INTO the Dorchester Hotel, your top reporter overheard an earth-shattering exchange between hotel steward and occidental member of a Japanese film crew.

"What exactly does Mr Zappa do?"

"Errr, he plays saxophone doesn't he?"

In light of this, Frank Zappa – over for four British dates – was never going to have an easy time at his press conference. But even this gave no hint of the ruthless stream-of-banality that threatened to thwart his every move.

In a furious first five minutes he was rattled by such toughies as, What made you decide to go back on tour? and, Could you tell us about your new album? I was stung into action, aware that if disaster was to be avoided I would have to take on the press conference single-handed.

Dutifully wheeling out the trusty, Is it true you once ate shit on stage? Mr Zappa was goaded into action.

"No, that isn't true but I will give you the stock answer I've given for the last 20 years: the nearest I've ever come to eating shit was at a Holiday Inn."

One of Frank's hot new numbers is 'Jesus Thinks You're A Jerk', a direct assault on TV evangelist and Republican presidential candidate Pat Robertson. Is Frank hoping he'll sue?

"Jesus or Pat?"

Ho ho!

"I say the same thing that I've said to all the major record companies: come and get me, make my day!"

Do you think your (legendarily fast) rendering of Stravinsky's 'Royal March' predicted speed metal?

Frank, missing the comical nature of my question: "No, because my rendering of the 'Royal March' come a long time after speed metal."

Nonetheless it is very fast.

"Oh yes, its fast. Wait'll you hear our version of Ravel's Bolero."

Can't wait, Frank.

FRANK: A pressing engagement

This Week's Albums

FRANK ZAPPA: 'Joes Garage, Parts I, II And III' (EMI) – Triple box set which is being made available for the first time in the UK, to coincide with Zappa's current tour.

FRANK ZAPPA: 'Shut Up 'N' Play Yer Guitar' (EMI) Another triple set: this one has been unavailable in this format for three years and is entirely composed of guitar instrumentals.

TO SON IT UP

MARY ANNE HOBBS on a day in the life of **DWEEZIL ZAPPA**, brother of Moon Unit, son of Frank and all-round guitar man

BROTHER OF Moon Unit. . . son of Frank, Dweezil Zappa reclines by the window of his five star Holland Park hotel suite, popping the odd strawberry.

"I hate clubs," he announces. "We went to the worst place on the planet last night. The gig reeked of the jet set. I was waiting for Robin Leach from *Lifestyles Of The Rich And Famous* to bowl in.

"It was *so* smoky in there, I was *amazed* that the fire alarm didn't go off. I mean, how do they tell when there's a fire in this town?" he asks in a resolute drawl.

"See, I don't drink, or smoke or dance or do drugs. . . "

What do you do, Dweezil?

"Play guitar. A normal *day in the life of*, is wake up, play guitar, have something to eat, play guitar, perhaps see a movie, play guitar, go to sleep."

And talk. It's difficult to slip one syllable between his frothing verbal torrent.

"When I was six," he continues voluntarily, "I really wanted to be a marine biologist, I was reading all these books about fish and stuff. Then I saw *Jaws*, which killed that idea stone dead."

At 12, Dweezil was performing with pa. A year later, he recorded his first single, 'My Mother Is A Space Cadet' (co-written with Steve Vai and produced by Eddie Van Halen).

He's done time VJ-ing with MTV, scored acting rolls in three major movies, cameoed on Don Johnson, Maria Vidal and Fat Boys' plastic, and is about to star with sister, Moon Unit, in a new TV comedy series.

Last week, Dweezil also released a promising album, 'My Guitar Wants To Kill Your Mama', (a title dredged from father's archives deliberately to provoke the PMRC).

He's the kind of all round Action-Boy that makes you wanna lose your breakfast.

"Nobody ever worked with me as a favour to my dad," he insists. "I think I've had it tougher than most people because I am the son of a famous person.

"My dad purposely stays out of my affairs. He only gets involved on the legal side, just to make sure I don't get screwed over.

"He's sued every record company on the planet, so he knows a bit about it!"

Do you ever worry that you may turn into a basket case like Michael Jackson, because of your 'distinguished' childhood?

"Hey, the moment I realise that I wanna buy the Elephant Man," he grins, "I'll start to panic."

DWEEZIL: MY father hates the PMRC

(Photo Credit: Erling Agergaard from Ole Lysgaard's Collection)

"Frank came in and gave Dweezil a big hug and told him that he was a musician now — because it was the most demanding backing that he had ever had to play a solo over. At least with Frank, and he pulled it off really well. Frank said it was great. It was a nice moment." — **Mike Keneally** (from Mike's Zappa Tour Diaries)

(Photo Credit: Milo Albonico)

(Photo Credit: Erling Agergaard from Ole Lysgaard's Collection)

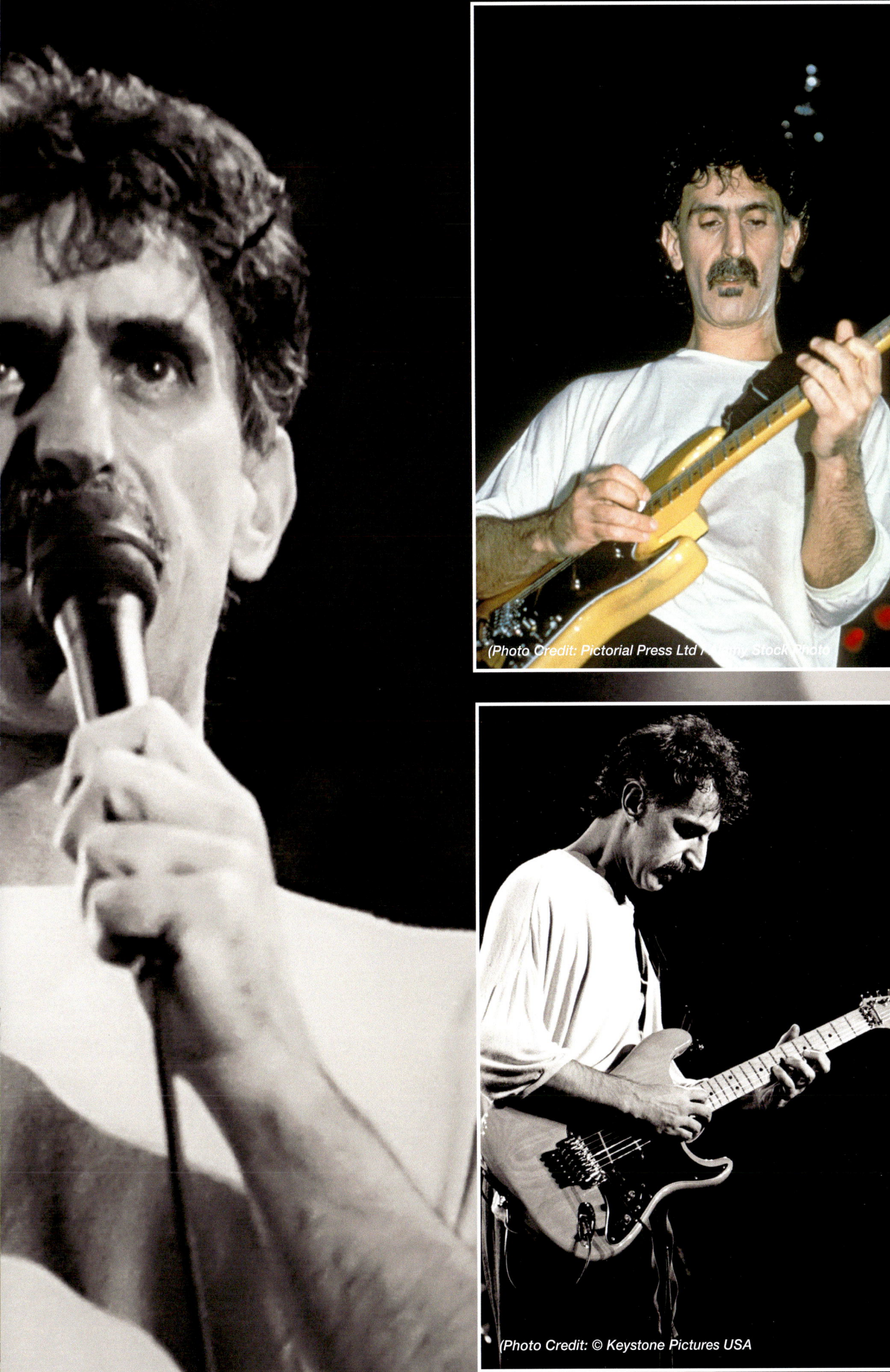

"It was cool because I met a lot of interesting people on the road. A lot of different types of characters that would follow the band around from gig to gig. Kind of like a lot of Dead-head types that would manage to scrape up enough money to get to the next gig. It was cool! You get to know a lot of people on the road and you see them at every gig. It made life interesting, and it made the tour go a lot easier because it became more of like... you felt like you had a road family. It was great!" — **Albert Wing** (from an interview with Fred Banta, March 2000)

(Photo Credit: Erling Agergaard from Ole Lysgaard's Collection)

"By the time the band got to Europe, the vibe within the organisation was terrible. Things got much worse with the addition of several English record company reps who seized upon the obviously bad band situation as kind of a game to play, in the form of creating and spreading rumours within the organisation that would serve only to increase the misery and friction." — **Ed Mann**
(from the book *Cosmik Debris: The Collected History And Improvisations Of Frank Zappa* by Greg Russo)

"We each got a picture laminate. Most of the time I'd take it off and leave it on the tech stand, so it wasn't dangling in front of me. I came back one night, and somebody had taken a very sharp object and jabbed my picture about ten times." — **Scott Thunes**

"We were at home, and a lot of people knew about us. The applause just got even louder as I walked Mats over to Bobby Martin's keyboards. Bobby said, 'Here's a Yamaha DX-9, and here is the Yamaha electric grand — good luck!' The band kept a reggae beat going during our entrance, which was good; now we could start our jam from the groove already going. I was in heaven because I could see Frank standing in front of the drum set with a BIG smile holding his conductor stick." — Morgan Ågren (from his website)

(Photo Credit: Børge Agergaard from Ole Lysgaard's Collection)

(Photo Credit: Erling Agergaard from Ole Lysgaard's Collection)

"Frank was beaming, and I was very deeply affected. I hadn't seen any kind of commitment to match this devotion to the music in a very long time, and it sort of reminded me what it was about. Very cool stuff. After Big Swifty, we went into Joe's Garage, which to me sounded horrible in comparison to those guys." — Mike Keneally (from Mike's Zappa Tour Diaries)

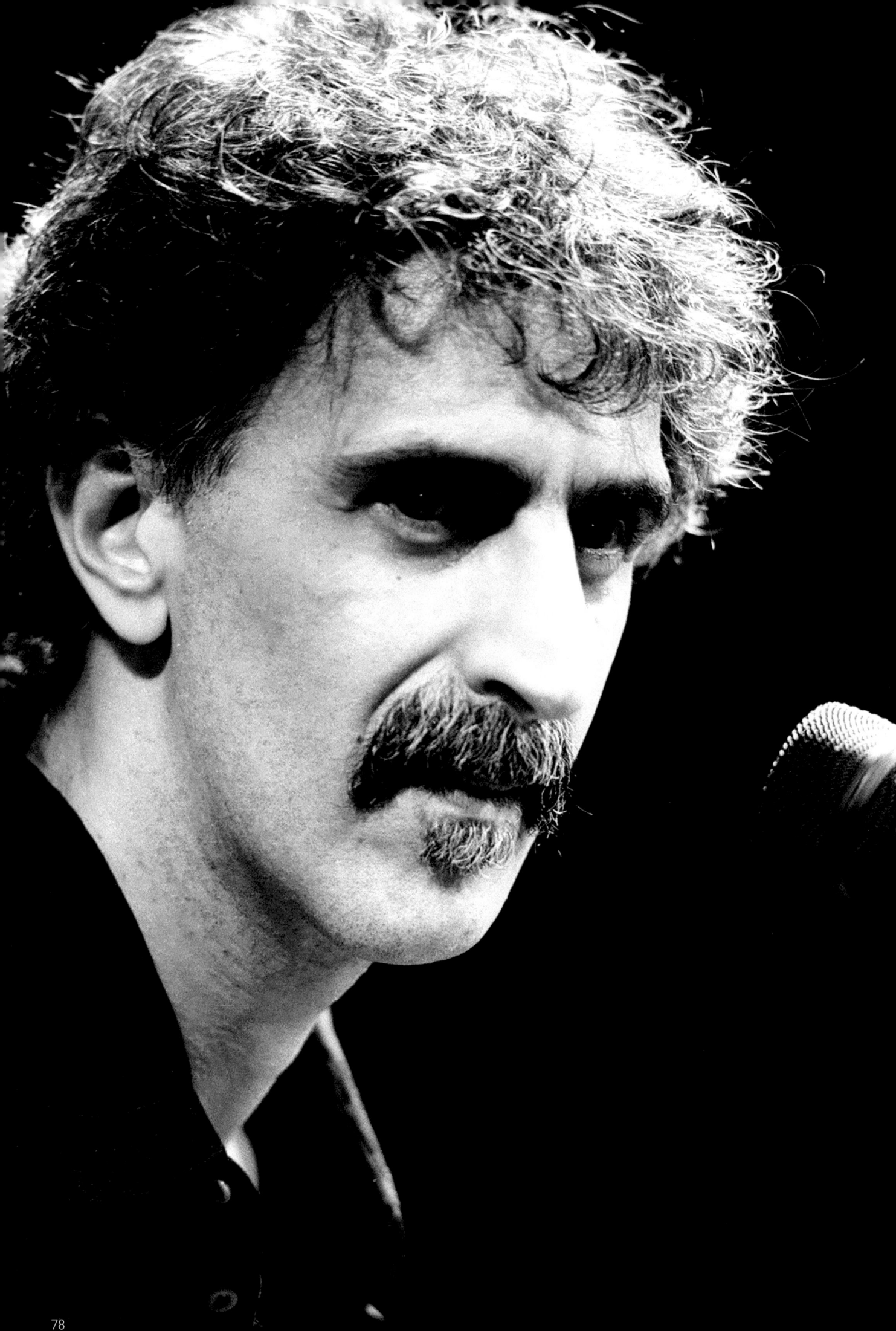

INTERVIEW WITH FRANK ZAPPA
BY PAULINE BUTCHER

This interview was conducted on 18 April 1988 at London's Hyde Park Hotel, hours before the first of two consecutive shows at the Wembley Arena, which I attended. I remember thinking (from my vantage point in the third row) how healthy Frank looked. Little did I know.

Pauline was Frank's secretary from 1968 to 1972. She was initially hired during The Mothers first European tour to transcribe the lyrics for *Absolutely Free* album. Frank then invited her to move out to his Laurel Canyon Boulevard home (The Log Cabin) where, among other things, she ran the United Mutations fan club.

In 2011, her memoir *Freak Out! My Life with Frank Zappa* was published by Plexus Books. The book documents her four-year experience living and working with Frank. It includes edited excerpts from this interview, which was recorded for local radio station 210, but was deemed too contentious for broadcast at the time.

Pauline has posted some audio extracts on YouTube, where you can hear Frank's constant coughs throughout, but this is the first time the complete interview has been published in one place.

I'm talking to Frank Zappa who's over here in London. I want to ask you first about the children, who are now grown up. When I last saw them they were tiny tots — in fact, two of them weren't even born.
That's really a tiny tot — that's a micro-tot.

That's right. Moon is, what, about twenty? She was four when I last saw her. What is she doing now?
Well, she has a boyfriend. She has her own house, and she and Dweezil have a deal with CBS television to do a pilot for a sitcom in the fall.[i]

So she's working in television?
Being an actress.

When did she move out?
Early this year.

So you have three of them living with you now?
Well, she's over at the house quite a bit anyway, even though she has her own place. But yeah, three of them are still there. We hardly see Dweezil because he has his own career and he is wandering around promoting his new album. In fact, he's here in London right now doing some work for MTV. And Ahmet, who I don't think you…

No, I didn't know him.
He's thirteen. And Diva is eight.
Ahmet is, er… let's be kind and describe him as a sex-crazed lunatic.

He takes after his father, does he?
[chuckles] Yes, he does. And I'm sure that Diva will eventually follow in her big brother's footsteps. She's very peculiar. I think she's psychic. We have a fax machine at the house where you just write something and it goes through a satellite to another place on the planet, and we were in Berlin and I got two drawings via a fax from the house: one of 'em was a comparative map of China versus Germany. And the other one said, "Happy Birthday," and it wasn't my birthday. But it turns out that it was my body-guard's birthday. I don't know how she could have known that but he was certainly amazed to see the drawings.[ii]

So what about Dweezil? Tell me a little bit more about him — he's making albums and playing the same kind of music as you?
He plays heavy metal. And he has a contract with Chrysalis. His new album is called *My Guitar Wants To Kill You Mama*.[iii]

And how old is he?
He's eighteen.

So you're not a parent to him anymore?
Oh, yeah, certainly — 'cos he still lives at the house.

And what sort of father are you?
Well, I could suggest you use your imagination. But [chuckles] I'm really pretty good.

Do you have any rules for the children — apart from no drugs in the house, which I know you've always had as a rule.
Well, they have to be in by a certain time, just like other parents would do with their kids. And I suppose it's especially important in Los Angeles for two reasons because LA is a dangerous city. And also because they have a curfew for kids under a certain age when they have to be in.

Under what age?
I think it's sixteen. They can't be out past 11 o'clock, so we have to keep an eye on Ahmet.

How can he be a sex-crazed fiend in the day when AIDS is so prevalent?
Well, let's describe the situation in the United States. The most recent statistic that I heard is that the main age bracket where people are being discovered with AIDS is 30 and above. There are children who are born to parents who had had it, but there is virtually no AIDS in the teenage category.

One of the best kept secrets in American television, and what's been going on in American television is a constant barrage of advertising about AIDS — every day on the news you see two or three stores about AIDS, and the whole thrust of it is designed to dissuade teenagers from having sex, when in fact that's one of the lowest risk groups. But the conservative government in the United States thinks that this is a wonderful opportunity to use the fear of catching a fatal disease to keep kids from having a good time.

So, I don't think that there's much of a risk at all for a person in the 13 year-old age bracket.

What about Moon and Dweezil's age?[iv]
The danger starts right around 30. That was the report I saw.

You say you're a good father and presumably they've nothing much to rebel against — which is different from your own environment when you grew up.
Yeah, well, one of the things that I do that's different from the way my parents raised me was that if they said no, it meant no, even if it didn't make any sense at all. And in our house, if I say no, and any one of the kids disagrees with it and they can logically prove that I'm wrong, they win.

I think that's a good way to teach kids to use logic and make them learn to negotiate. I think that's something that ought to be developed in homes.

I try to do that myself with my son. But your parents were conventional, weren't they? What was it about your parents, do you think, that made you the way you are?
Not very much, because basically when you get to a point and you see that you parents are behaving in a way that is either illogical or irrelevant, then you may not wish to argue with them, or you don't want to hurt them because they have been nice to you. So you just ignore them and find your own way.

I think that if I would have followed every rule that was in the house when I grew up, I would be like them [little chuckle], and I wouldn't have had a very good time.

Right. Let's play a piece of music now — let's play *The Jazz Discharge Party Hats* from *The Man From Utopia*.[v]
I think that would be a very good thing for this audience to hear.

***

What can you tell me about that?
Well, the song was improvised during a concert at the Southern Illinois University and it's a

true story that happened to some of the guys in the band when we played in Albuquerque, New Mexico.

There is a tradition in the band that if something of a folklore nature occurs that is worth passing on to the audience, I will find some way of doing it during the show. There will be an explanation spoken with a musical accompaniment – or, in this case, a sort of improvised jazz, sort of song.

The way this track was done was, I improvised the words and the melody line and the band improvised the accompaniment and then, before it went on to the record, Steve Vai transcribed the melody line that I sang and doubled it on the guitar.

So the net result is kind of like a very perverted version of a George Benson record.

When did you realise that music was going to be the dominant force in your life?
About the time I was eighteen.

That's pretty late: Mozart started when he was four.
Yeah, but he lived in Austria, didn't he?[vi] Living in the United States and living in a household like I had, there wasn't even a record player in the house until I was 15. So I couldn't even hear any music unless it was on the radio, and what they were playing on the radio in those days was things like *(How Much Is) That Doggie in the Window?* — that kind of stuff. That's not really a rich musical heritage upon which to draw.

Let's talk about your instrumental music. When you compose that, do you still do it the same way as you did when I was there — I remember you tinkling around on the piano and working out the tunes and melodies that way, and then filling them in.
Well, I do it two ways now. Like right now, here in the hotel, I don't have a piano. I tried to rent one, but it was too ungodly expensive. So I just sit over there and write it out and take it to the next soundcheck or rehearsal with the band, and pass out the parts and play it right away.

If I'm at home, I have a machine called the Synclavier which allows me to write the music, push a button, and it plays it back automatically.

I see that you can't resist having provocative titles: one of your instrumentals is called *G-Spot Tornado*. How did that title come about?
I thought it was a good name for a song. And apparently, I was right. A lot of people listen to that song and say, "Yeah, that's a good name for that song." Unfortunately, the station that you work for probably doesn't even have a copy of *G-Spot Tornado*.

Which album is it from?
Jazz From Hell.[vii]

No, I don't think they do. Let's play something else – let's play *Lucille* from *Joe's Garage*[viii].
That's a good idea.

***

What can you tell me about that one?
That was originally written for the Jeff Simmons[ix] album I produced about 1969, and that album went nowhere. But I thought it was a good song, so I built into it the storyline of *Joe's Garage* so that eventually somebody would get to hear the song.

Are you happy about the way your instrumental music has gone from strength to strength over the years?
Some of it has turned out pretty good. Other parts haven't. But that's to be expected, I guess.

Do you still get your music played by symphony orchestras?
If I pay them.

And is that worth it?
No.

So you don't do that very often?
That's right.

81

I want to talk about the songs themselves now. The lyrics that you write upset quite a lot of people. Do you not feel tempted sometimes to put some acceptable words on to some of your pretty tunes, and thereby get them played on the radio and get yourself a bit more money?
I think it's too late for anything like that! I have no inclination to do it. If you want to hear a nice little tune with empty little words, there's plenty of other people that will write that for ya. And there's no reason to crowd that particular market place.

Right. Even though you don't get your music played on a lot of stations in the States, you still manage to sell a lot of records?
Still in business.

How does that work, though. Where do they get the information — from concerts?
From concerts, from the interviews I do. And the fact that we sell a lot of products through mail order, direct mail.

How many records must you have made now? I see that in 1978/79, you put out four records, which is quite a lot. I don't know if that was a backlog building up, and then about fifteen in the last twenty years, right? About one every eighteen months?
Well, I've been in the business for twenty-three years and there's about fifty albums… fifty or fifty-one.

So any Frank Zappa buff ought to have fifty-one albums in their library?
At least, yeah.

And they're collector's items some of those, I imagine.
That's true.

I want to ask you a hypothetical question now. Supposing you were in prison and in order to get out you had to write eight songs in praise of eight different things, or eight different people — as opposed to what you do in most of your songs, which is parody, satire, criticise and so on — if you had to do that, would you…
If I had to do it? Only Pauline Butcher would come up with a question like this! A lot would depend on how bad the prison was.

Off the top of your head, can you think of nothing that you would praise — something that's good in this world?
Oh, I think there are many things that are good in this world. But I don't think they're so good I'd write a song about 'em.

Nothing at all?
No.

Okay. Let's play *Crew Slut* from *Joe's Garage*. What are you going to tell me about that?
It's also based on characters from real life. The girls that are being described in the song, they do exist. Every rock and roll band, and every rock and roll crew, knows that there is a species of crew slut lurking out there who live for the privilege of doing the laundry and performing other services for men who put up the PA system and focus the lights on stage. And this song is in praise of them, Pauline. In praise of the crew sluts.

***

That was *In Praise Of The Crew Sluts* from *Joe's Garage* by Frank Zappa.
   Now, what political issues have you been involved in most recently? I know you've always had a crusade against drugs, and you've written many songs about that and a few other issues you've been involved in. What is your latest interest?
I've been concerned about the rise of fundamentalist religion in the United States and in the way in which it has interfered with legislation in American politics. That's all.
   Maybe you don't realise that the First Amendment to the United States Constitution guarantees a separation between church and state, and during the Reagan administration, that dividing line has been somewhat blurred, and when you have people who want to convert

religious dogma into legislation at the expense of other people's beliefs, I think that's a bad way of doing business. And so I've been pretty outspoken against that since Reagan got into office.

What can you actually do to make any changes in that area?
Well, for one thing, most people in the United States are afraid to speak out on it because they don't want to be perceived as anti-religious, and that has never bothered me, since one of the things that I've always maintained is that most of the problems in the world today could be cured if we nuked the clergy.

Have you had anything to say about Pat Robertson?[xi]
Yeah, we have several songs about Pat. Fortunately his presidential campaign went nowhere, though he spent more money than all the rest of the guys. I think that it's a good indication that there's still a few sane people left in the United States.

But there isn't an evangelist of that sort who is President, so they do have limited political power, do they not? Or am I misunderstanding the issue?
You have to understand that Pat Robertson was a television evangelist who was taking in 253 million dollars a year for the last decade, tax free; close personal friends with Ronald Reagan; big contributor to Republican Party candidates for Congress; probably involved with funding for the secret war in Nicaragua; close personal friend of Oliver North; and, as far as I'm concerned, guilty of tax avoidance of the highest magnitude because the television show that he claimed as a religious ministry was nothing more than political propaganda, and the law in the United States that gives broadcast evangelists the right to do their business tax free, states very clearly that to keep their tax exemption, they may not lobby for or against any political candidate or for or against any legislation.

Basically, his programme has been all political lobbying, and the Internal Revenue Service in the United States that regulates these activities, has been somewhat lax in prosecuting this violation partly because the IRS is under the jurisdiction of the Secretary of the Treasury, a man named Baker[xii] who happens to be a Born Again Christian.

So you have the entire Reagan administration infested with these types who are looking out for each other and they've made a fortune, tax free, just like the defence contractors have made a fortune, tax free, during the last seven years of Reagan.

Now, all of a sudden, this man decides he's going to run for President and he's going to use the influence he's developed over the years with close personal friends in Washington DC and capitalise on this slush fund that he's built up from his television ministry and everybody thought that he was really going to make a dent in American politics. But he didn't do very much at all, which is good news.

We don't really have that same problem here.
Well, wait just a minute: I saw a bus going by on the street the other day, talking about Jesus's Army. What is this stuff?

I don't know. There's a few small things of that kind, but they haven't really got an edgeway as yet into the media or into television.
Yeah, well, it takes them a while before they save up enough money to buy television time, like Robertson. These guys started off in tent show, just doing little live things, and the very idea of a Jesus Army claiming that it's going to fight for you, that Jesus's Army has the heart to fight for you. What is this stuff? It's like Fascism with a cross.

Why do you think these people have such a following?
Well, the biggest push that these television ministries had in the last seven years was during that part of the Reagan administration when we had a depression in the United States — 'cos during troubled economic times, people have a tendency to reach out for mystical solutions to practical problems and when they've lost all other forms of hope, a man comes along and says if you'll just send me a donation, then Jesus will hear your prayer and your problems will be solved.

There are many people in the US that are stupid enough to believe that and I'll guarantee you that if we had another depression in the United States there'd be another whole batch of these guys saying send me the money and only then will Jesus hear your prayer and everything will be fine. And looking at that sign on the bus yesterday leads me to believe that you've got the same sort of racket ready to occur in Great Britain.

Yes, but hopefully it won't take over in the same way.
Well, you have to keep your eye on them, 'cos these guys are nasty little crooks.

Let's play another piece of music now. Let's play *Cocaine Decisions* from *The Man From Utopia*. Can you tell me something about that?
Yeah. I've done quite a few songs against drugs and here is an example of an anti-drug song that should have gotten a lot of airplay in the United States during the time when people were saying, *"Well, we should do more against drugs,"* and this song was completely overlooked.

***

I notice you have a lot more security around you now than you used to twenty years ago when I was with you. Why is that necessary?
Because in 1971, when I was playing at the Rainbow here I was attacked on stage. I'd never carried a bodyguard prior to that time. I was attacked on the stage and I was injured pretty badly and I had to spend the rest of the year in a wheelchair. And so from that point on, I started carrying security rather than let the local promoters supply it.

You're now forty-seven years old. In three years' time, you'll be fifty — half-way to a hundred. Do you find touring very tiring now?
I've found touring very tiring for a long time. Travelling is the part that I dislike the most. I still like to play, but it's especially difficult when you come to Europe because going through customs, the airline schedules are not as extensive as they are in the United States, you don't have the choice of flights when you can leave any time you want, and you wind up getting up too early in the morning. So you spend two months over here on five or six hours sleep a night. And that can run you down.

Your fans used to be mostly university students, as I recall when I was working with you. What's happened to your fan situation now? Are they the same students who are nearly fifty years old now, or are they still university students?
Well, let's take a peculiar example like last night's concert in Brighton. The audience was skinheads, punks, weekend beachgoers… whoever those people are that go to Brighton for an amazing Saturday night experience. They were quite mixed. They were quite young. They were very drunk. And there was one guy who was pressed right up to the barricade in the front who was vomiting, which is a little tough to watch while you're singing.

    But to think of this audience as fifty year-old ex-college students would be a big mistake. First of all, older people tend not to go to concerts because they don't want to have vomit on their shoes, and younger people tend to go to concerts no matter who's playing.

You wouldn't sell out your concerts if you didn't have the following here though.
Well, I presume that somebody in this country likes what I do because there's some fan mail there, you can read it… I think we have an audience in this country, in spite of what the British pop press have tried to do over the years.

Now we're going to play another record. This is one with the, er, squashed éclair…
It's from *The Jazz Discharge Party Hats*.

On that, it's got, "She passed me her pants, and in the bottom it was like a squashed éclair."
Well, that's not an exact quote. I think probably what's on the song is even worse than that.[xiii] But that's true: that's what it was.

Yes, but that sort of thing upsets people, doesn't it.
[pause] No.

It does.
It doesn't upset Americans.

Well, that's why they won't play it — they won't play the record if that's got that sort of words on it.
Squashed éclair?

Yes. We won't go into it, Frank. [laughs] I don't get upset by it, because I know you and I know that you mean it as a joke, as amusing and as satirical comment…
You mean that if a known criminal were to write those words, they would be taken differently?

Absolutely, yes.
You mean, like Ed Meese?[xiv] If he said there was a squashed éclair in the bottom of her pants, people would perceive that in a different way?

They would perceive him as being a lot different from what he is. And they would probably perceive you as somewhat different from what you are.
I'm a reporter. I saw a squashed éclair in the bottom of the girl's underpants. So I should tell people about that and perhaps warn them of the dangers of wearing such things, you know? [little chuckle] What if it festered? [both laugh]
    I mean, I don't eat them. I don't play with them. But I do observe them. So I'm just the messenger here.

But you obviously put it into your song because you know it will have a provocative effect.
No, I put it into the song because people need to know these things.

Why? Who needs to know about a squashed éclair at the bottom of someone's pants?
Well, let me put it to you this way: perhaps there are young men out there that have the idea that women are something different from what they actually are. Believe it or not, there are girls in this world who walk around with pants that do have a squashed éclair in the bottom. We should be blunt about it.

[laughing] Are you speaking literally, or metaphorically?
No, that's all just literally. I mean, not a real squashed éclair, but material that would resemble the components of an éclair – that is, the custard, the chocolate and perhaps some of the flaky crust material.

Well, now *I'm* shocked!
Why? You may be one of the fortunate people who doesn't know anyone who wears pants like that. But let me just say that in travelling around the world, playing rock and roll, you can meet people who have this going for them.
[laughter]

Let's play something more sedate. How about *Tink Walks Amok*?[xv]
That's very sedate. *Tink Walks Amok* is a tribute to Arthur Barrow who was the bass player in the band for quite some time, and Tink is his nickname — although he wouldn't like people to know, but that's what they used to call him when he was in school in San Antonio, Texas. And 'walking amok' is like 'running amuck'; it's a bass player's walk.

I have one last question. Is there anything you would like to ask me?
[pause for thought] Not on the tape. [laughter] Wait a minute. There is one thing. You remember that time we were at your house and you were washing your hair?

Yes.
What were you really doing with that hairbrush?

I beg your pardon! I was probably brushing my hair.
Ooooh — I don't know, Pauline!
[hearty laughter]

Well, we will call it a day now, Frank. It was lovely talking to you, thank you very much.
Okay.

[i] *Normal Life,* starring Moon and Dweezil, aired from March 21 until July 18, 1990. Dweezil told the author, *"Originally it was gonna be like The Adams Family: you could do anything within the house, because it would be considered normal by the family. 'Normal' people would come over and be considered weird based on the precedent for normal inside the house. But the network flipped it on us — they said, "Let's make you really normal and have the neighbours be wacky!" We were glad to see it dropped because we hated working on it. We hated the people; they were just the most pathetic bunch of fucking losers ever."*

[ii] In 2019, after studying *"many different modalities of working with energy,"* Diva is certified in Reiki and Restorative Yoga, and is *"an intuitive tarot reader."*

[iii] This was the follow-up to Dweezil's 1986 debut album, *Havin' A Bad Day*, which was produced by Frank. This album takes its title from one of Frank's compositions and features performances by Scott Thunes, Terry Bozzio and brother Ahmet.

[iv] At the time of this interview, Moon was 20.

[v] Zappa album, released in 1983.

[vi] Wolfgang Amadeus Mozart was born in 1756 in the capital of the Archbishopric of Salzburg, an ecclesiastic principality in what is now Austria, but was then part of the Holy Roman Empire.

[vii] Released in 1986.

[viii] *Joe's Garage Act I*, released in 1979.

[ix] Zappa's bass player/guitarist from 1969 to 1974. Zappa co-produced Simmons' 1970 debut album *Lucille Has Messed My Mind Up* under the pseudonym La Marr Bruister.

[x] Ronald Wilson Reagan (1911–2004), who served as the 40th President of the United States from 1981 to 1989. Prior to the presidency, he was a Hollywood actor and union leader before serving as the 33rd Governor of California from 1967 to 1975.

[xi] Former Republican presidential candidate and Southern Baptist minister who advocates a conservative Christian ideology.

[xii] James Addison Baker III

[xiii] *"...one of the guys from the band picked up her panties. He told me later that the stuff in the bottom was like punching an éclair..."*

[xiv] Edwin Meese III, a friend of Ronald Reagan's who served in a number of official capacities within the Republican Party, eventually rising to hold the position of the 75th Attorney General of the United States (1985–1988). In 1984, Meese was investigated for giving out Government jobs in exchange for financial assistance, and was accused of passing legislation to aid his suspect dealings.

[xv] Also from *The Man From Utopia* album.

Photo by Jay Petitt

"It was the second show in Rotterdam where the band really let me down. They really started to play wrong notes. Inexcusable wrong notes. And I started talking about 'maybe we should rehearse more.' And for two or three days everybody had their nose out of joint like I have no right to tell them that they're playing wrong notes. And in Europe people listen to the notes." —
Frank Zappa
(from an interview with Den Simms, Eric Buxton and Rob Samler, December 1989)

"Frank wanted to do Boléro. I found the sheet music, and I'm sitting there looking at it and Paul Carman asked me if he could see it. I said 'Fuck off. Get your own.' And anybody who knows me at all, they know how to deal with it. Chad would've gone, 'Oh, come on! Lemme see it,' and I would've handed it to him. But Paul... I have no use for anybody who has no use for me. If the only reason you want to talk to me is to see my sheet music, fuck off!" — **Scott Thunes** (from the book *In Cold Sweat: Interviews With Really Scary Musicians* by Thomas Wictor)

"Scott, you've got to stop doing this, man. You've gotta stop; you're pissing too many people off. Stop!" — **Ike Willis**

"This cake had all the band members' names in frosting on it, and somebody had taken a knife and drawn a nice little inch-deep line through my name. And of course the best thing would have been to walk away. But I took a spoon, and I scooped out Ed Mann's and Chad Wackerman's names. I played back into their hands. I should not have done it, and I didn't enjoy it." — **Scott Thunes** (from the book *In Cold Sweat: Interviews With Really Scary Musicians* by Thomas Wictor)

"For those of you who might not know... the whole is the sum of its parts. For those of you who might not know... no single part can be a whole all by itself, unless it's a fucking black hole. For those of you who might not know, belligerence is obnoxious. For those of you who might not know... the Nazis were never that popular anyway!" — **Ed Mann** (on stage in Pennsylvania, March 1988)

"At the end of the huddle we always held before the gig, I uncharacteristically fell back into Clonemeister garb to say about some piece of music that was being incorrectly played by some or all of the band. I said something like, 'For those of you who might not know, the last chord is an F#.' It must have been something important for me to even speak to those guys at all. So Ed slung my own words back in my face. Ouch!" — **Scott Thunes**

"Looking back, I cannot understand why I did not quit early on — FZ or not." — **Ed Mann**

"I've found touring very tiring for a long time. I still like to play, but it's especially difficult when you come to Europe because the airline schedules are not as extensive as they are in the United States and you wind up getting up too early in the morning. You spend two months over here on five or six hours sleep a night, and that can run you down." — **Frank Zappa** (from an interview with Pauline Butcher, April 1988)

"Mike Keneally and I had been drinking champagne — we were gettin' pretty drunk. And Bruce Fowler would not shut up. So I stood up, and I dropped my pants, and I stood with my cock and balls three inches in front of his face. He sat there for thirty seconds, and he got up. And that was it. They left me alone from that point on. But nobody ever tried to understand my point of view." — **Scott Thunes** (from the book *In Cold Sweat: Interviews With Really Scary Musicians* by Thomas Wictor)

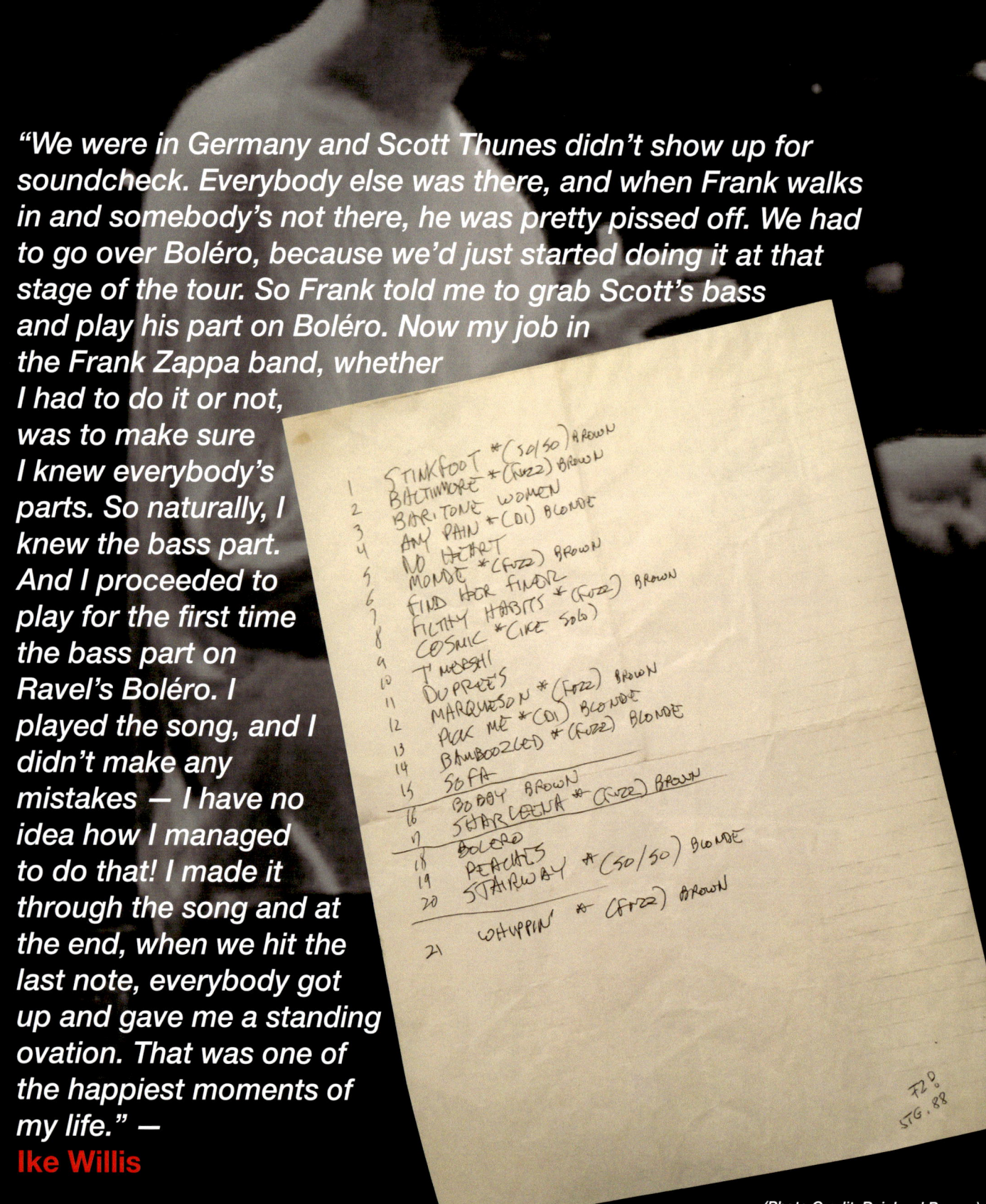

"We were in Germany and Scott Thunes didn't show up for soundcheck. Everybody else was there, and when Frank walks in and somebody's not there, he was pretty pissed off. We had to go over Boléro, because we'd just started doing it at that stage of the tour. So Frank told me to grab Scott's bass and play his part on Boléro. Now my job in the Frank Zappa band, whether I had to do it or not, was to make sure I knew everybody's parts. So naturally, I knew the bass part. And I proceeded to play for the first time the bass part on Ravel's Boléro. I played the song, and I didn't make any mistakes — I have no idea how I managed to do that! I made it through the song and at the end, when we hit the last note, everybody got up and gave me a standing ovation. That was one of the happiest moments of my life." —
Ike Willis

(Photo Credit: Reinhard Preuss)

(Photo Credit: Reinhard Preuss)

"Frank told me on the bus ride to Copenhagen that he'd written a Johnny Cash-type song for me to sing. Bob Rice kept telling me how that was a big step — to have a song written especially for you – and I'm sure that's true." — Mike Keneally
(from Mike's Zappa Tour Diaries)

"I've heard more kinds of music than the average listener today. I lived through a whole musical area that most of the fans that listen to it now, they never heard those songs. So things that would seem automatic to me, as a visual aid so to speak, you'll never know. I mean, you've probably never even heard Mississippi Mud. One day, in an old movie, you'll hear that song, and you'll go, 'Uh-oh! It's Rhymin' Man'" — Frank Zappa
from an interview with Den Simms, Eric Buxton and Rob Samler,

"Chad wore sunglasses during rehearsals. For the lights. Not always. But the lights bothered him sometimes." — **Sergio Albonico**

"According to the man himself, eye protection worn at every gig in 1988 was because he had a broken-drumstick mishap at some point and had eye surgery to repair said damage. He figured an ounce of prevention was worth never having such a terrible thing happen to him again." — **Scott Thunes**
(post at www.zappateers.com, December 2015)

"At the end of the tour, Frank was in so much pain and discomfort that he could not pee without holding his hand under warm water. He often could not stand up immediately, was often holding his gut and doubled over in pain. He told me before we even left LA how sick he was." —
Unnamed band member to author's friend

(Photo Credit: Erling Agergaard from Ole Lysgaard's Collection)

"During the course of the concert, I remember Frank changed a few lyrics, the upshot suggesting it was over for the band." — Albert Wing

"If it had been a different day and Frank was in a different mood I'm sure the band would have continued with another bass player. It just occurred when Frank was in a bad mood and woke up on the wrong side of the cave. He was just starting to get sick and he just said fuck it." —
Ike Willis
(from an interview with A.J. Abrams, March, 2000)

"Frank got on the bus with the horn section and asked them if they would perform with Scott. They said no, and simultaneously Frank asked the Fowlers if they could get in touch with Tom to see if he would do it. He said yes — then they too never heard another word about it."
— **Ed Mann**

(Photo Credit: Erling Agergaard from Ole Lysgaard's Collection)

"After the last show of the tour, Frank invited each member of the band in turn to join him in his dressing room. When I came in he said, 'Well, that's it. I want to do a six-piece band', and told me who was gonna be in it [Zappa, Keneally, Thunes, Ray White, Morgan Ågren and Mats Öberg]. He was very enamoured by Mats & Morgan after hearing them in Stockholm, and he wanted to check my availability. I said, 'I'll be there.' But his health took a turn for the worse and it didn't happen." — **Mike Keneally**

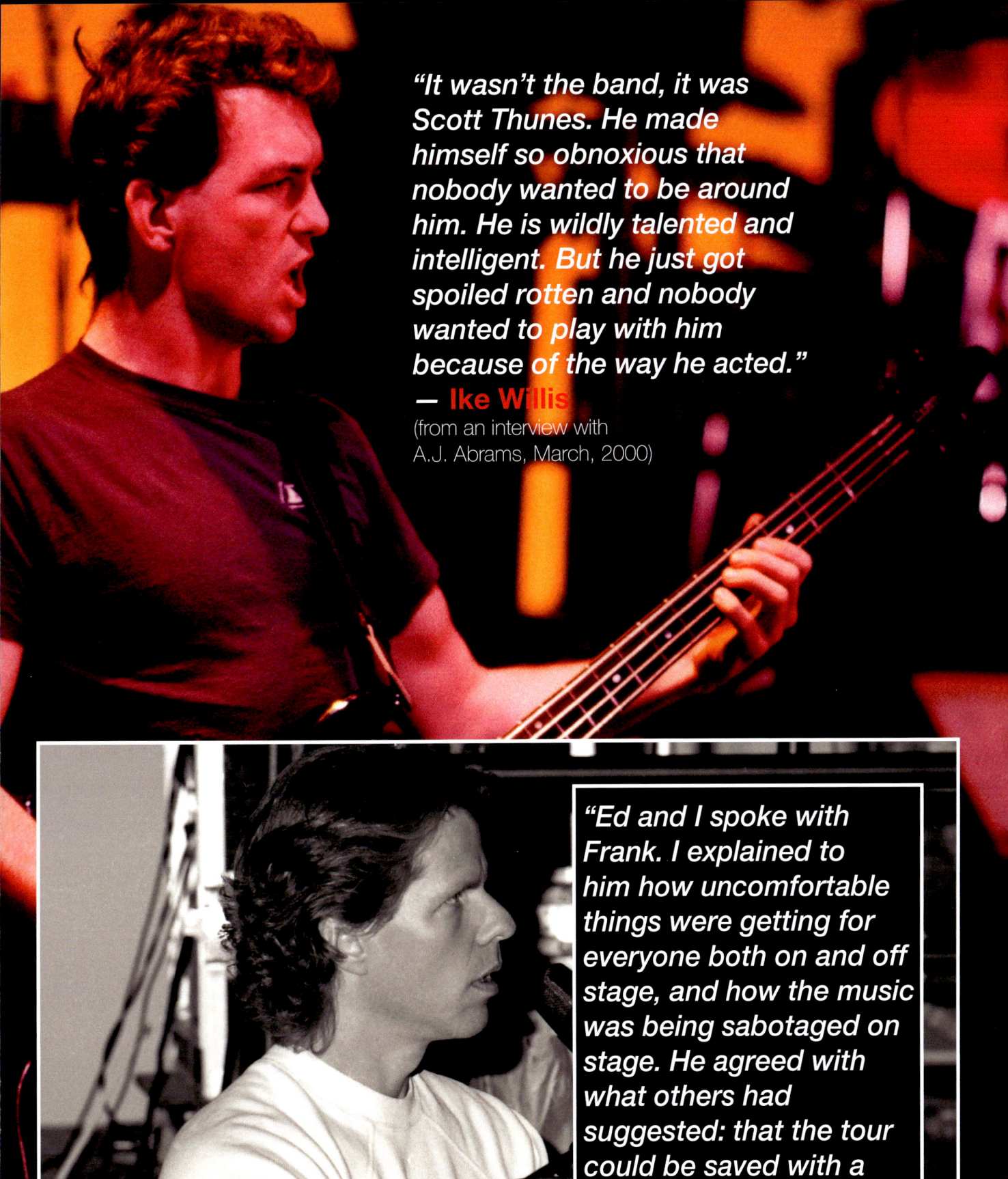

"It wasn't the band, it was Scott Thunes. He made himself so obnoxious that nobody wanted to be around him. He is wildly talented and intelligent. But he just got spoiled rotten and nobody wanted to play with him because of the way he acted."
— **Ike Willis**
(from an interview with A.J. Abrams, March, 2000)

"Ed and I spoke with Frank. I explained to him how uncomfortable things were getting for everyone both on and off stage, and how the music was being sabotaged on stage. He agreed with what others had suggested: that the tour could be saved with a personnel change." —
Robert Martin

"He looked at me for the longest time, because my face was very similar to his! He suddenly understood what kind of person I was, and what kind of music I preferred. I explained that I was a blues musician, a harp player. He laughed, and said 'Don't speak anymore; I think I know you very well!'" — **Fabio Treves**

Photos by Maki Galimberti

"Frank asked me if it was possible to organise a meeting with Paolo Pillitteri, the Mayor of Milan, asking if his opera, Dio Fa, could be staged at La Scala." — **Fabio Treves**

(Photo Credit: Erling Agergaard from Ole Lysgaard's Collection)

(Photo Credit: Erling Agergaard from Ole Lysgaard's Collection)

(Photo Credit: Erling Agergaard from Ole Lysgaard's Collection)

"At first, I was enjoying playing the guitar again. On a good night, the ideas I had for guitar solos came out. On a bad night, it was me versus the band. The audience didn't really know, but it was another example of the kind of thing that made me want to put the guitar down in the first place." — **Frank Zappa**
(from an interview with Alan di Perna, September 1988)

"Unfortunately his health was starting to fail and he was getting slower in making decisions. It was very sad." — **Mark Pinske**

in Genoa, Italy." —
Frank Zappa
(from an interview with
Charles Amirkhanian, April 1991)

"I always presumed his energy was not up to it, as I had seen so much of that in the previous twelve weeks. When this 'cancelled tour' got so much press, my true inner feeling was that Frank was using that to cover that he did not feel up to it; touring was his life. I found out nine months later that he was undergoing diagnoses." — Ed Mann

"The band realised they provided for themselves total unemployment. Everybody on that tour got paid but me. Within six months I was hearing, 'Man, we made a mistake. Scott's not such a bad guy.' It was just like little children ganging up on a kid at school. If that band had stayed together, not only would it be the most outrageous touring band on the planet, but I'd still be playing guitar. One of the sax players who'd been complaining that Scott didn't give him enough support on his solos, after he heard The Best Band You Never Heard In Your Life, he came over here and said, 'Oh, he sounds good, man.' Stuff like that makes me sick." —
Frank Zappa (from an interview with Matt Resnicoff, November 1991)

"My main problem with the situation was that it was affecting the music negatively. Although I know he respected my opinion, I also know he felt pressured, as if it were a mutiny, and finally cancelled the tour rather than be pushed by the band to make a change. I had a good relationship with Scott, I think largely because he respected my classical background. But the music was the most important thing. I wish I could have convinced him to act differently in the way he related to other band members." — **Robert Martin**

"It was Chad's fury with Scott — and my willingness to be a voice for it — that fuelled the fire from day one. My quibble with Scott was his willingness on a daily basis to treat these great musicians as shit on mic over a huge PA for hours on end. Chad is nice — genteel. Scott was fucking with everyone musically onstage by intentionally jumping beats. The music from the bass matched the body language from Scott at the time of execution. Very difficult to play with." — **Ed Mann**

   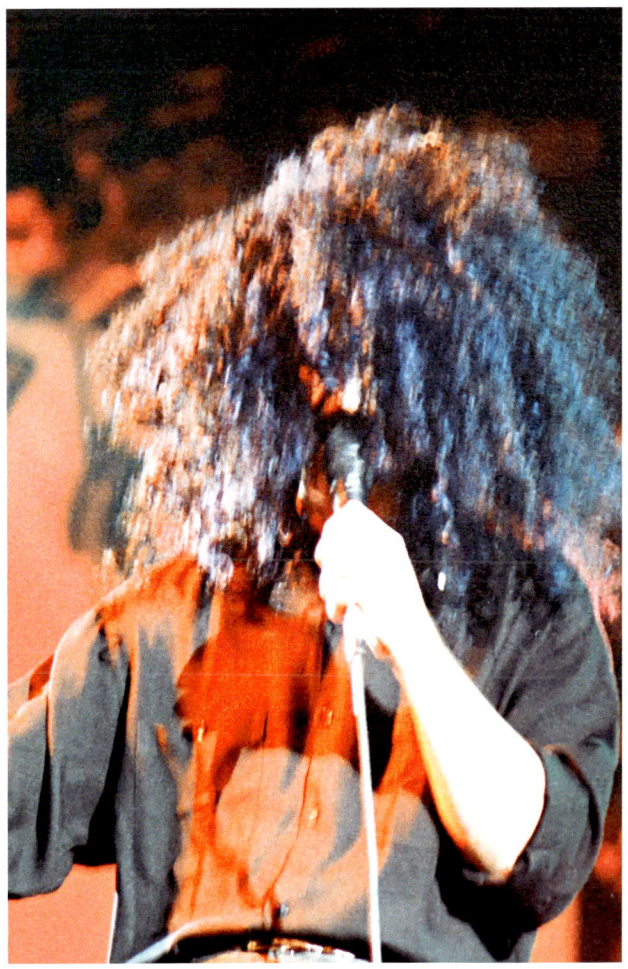

(Photo Credit: Erling Aagergaard from Ole Lysgaard's Collection)

"If I were half as fucking annoying to them as they were to me, then yes, I should bend over and gladly accept all ass-kickings. But I do not think it ever — during rehearsals — added up to abuse. The Jazzholes were sloppy, selfish, late, careless, annoying, and outside any manner of looking out for Frank's best interests. Yes, I have regrets. I'm no angel. But as Clonemeister, I was amazing. Fuck those guys." — **Scott Thunes**

"The 1988 tour would have been my absolute favourite tour, only the people who were managing Frank at the time were not my favourite people. The 1988 tour — as far as the band was concerned — was the most fun." — Ike Willis
(from an interview with the Evil Prince, 1996)

The Official FZ 88 Discography

Broadway The Hard Way

Official Release #53. Originally Released: October 25, 1988

Tracklisting:

01. Elvis Has Just Left The Building (2:24)
02. Planet Of The Baritone Women (2:48)
03. Any Kind Of Pain (5:42)
04. Dickie's Such An Asshole (5:45)
05. When The Lie's So Big (3:38)
06. Rhymin' Man (3:50)
07. Promiscuous (2:02)
08. The Untouchables (2:26)
09. Why Don't You Like Me? (2:57)
10. Bacon Fat (1:29)
11. Stolen Moments (2:58)
12. Murder By Numbers (5:37)
13. Jezebel Boy (2:27)
14. Outside Now (7:49)
15. Hot Plate Heaven At The Green Hotel (6:40)
16. What Kind Of Girl? (3:16)
17. Jesus Thinks You're A Jerk (9:16)

Notes: Album originally released on vinyl and cassette in October 1988 minus tracks 9-16, but with an additional 'confinement loaf' intro rap at the start of *Dickie's Such An Asshole* from the 12 February Philadelphia show. Expanded CD version released May 25, 1989.

The Best Band You Never Heard In Your Life

Official Release #55. Originally Released: April 16, 1991

Tracklisting:

DISC 1

01. Heavy Duty Judy (6:04)
02. Ring Of Fire (2:00)
03. Cosmik Debris (4:32)
04. Find Her Finer (2:42)
05. Who Needs The Peace Corps? (2:40)
06. I Left My Heart In San Francisco (0:36)
07. Zomby Woof (5:41)
08. Bolero (5:19)
09. Zoot Allures (7:07)
10. Mr. Green Genes (3:40)
11. Florentine Pogen (7:11)
12. Andy (5:51)
13. Inca Roads (8:19)
14. Sofa #1 (2:49)

DISC 2

01. Purple Haze (2:27)
02. Sunshine Of Your Love (2:30)
03. Let's Move To Cleveland (5:51)
04. When Irish Eyes Are Smiling (0:46)
05. "Godfather Part II" Theme (0:30)
06. A Few Moments With Brother A. West (4:01)
07. The Torture Never Stops Part One (5:20)
08. Theme From "Bonanza" (0:28)
09. Lonesome Cowboy Burt (Swaggart Version) (4:54)
10. The Torture Never Stops Part Two (10:47)
11. More Trouble Every Day (Swaggart Version) (5:28)
12. Penguin In Bondage (Swaggart Version) (5:05)
13. The Eric Dolphy Memorial Barbecue (9:18)
14. Stairway To Heaven (9:20)

Notes: Some early European releases of this album omitted *Bolero* because the estate of Maurice Ravel objected to Zappa's treatment of the song. In Japan, the album featured the above artwork by Cal Schenkel, used worldwide for the 1995 Rykodisc reissue, as Zappa had used a band picture on the original US and European version without the photographer's permission. The 2012 Universal Music Enterprises re-release reverts back to the original artwork, minus the ban(ne)d picture.

You Can't Do That On Stage Anymore, Vol. 4

Official Release #56. Originally Released: June 14, 1991

Tracklisting:

DISC 1

14. Take Me Out To The Ball Game (3:01)
15. Filthy Habits (5:39)

Make A Jazz Noise Here

Official Release #57. Originally Released: June 4, 1991

Tracklisting:

DISC 1

01. Stink-Foot (7:39)
02. When Yuppies Go To Hell (13:28)
03. Fire And Chains (5:04)
04. Let's Make The Water Turn Black (1:36)
05. Harry, You're A Beast (0:47)
06. The Orange County Lumber Truck (0:41)
07. Oh No (4:43)
08. Theme From Lumpy Gravy (1:11)
09. Eat That Question (1:54)
10. Black Napkins (6:56)
11. Big Swifty (11:12)
12. King Kong (13:04)
13. Star Wars Won't Work (3:40)

DISC 2

01. The Black Page (New Age Version) (6:45)
02. T'Mershi Duween (1:42)
03. Dupree's Paradise (8:34)
04. City Of Tiny Lights (8:01)
05. Royal March From "L'Histoire Du Soldat" (0:59)
06. Theme From The Bartok Piano Concerto #3 (0:43)
07. Sinister Footwear 2nd mvt. (6:39)
08. Stevie's Spanking (4:25)
09. Alien Orifice (4:15)
10. Cruisin' For Burgers (8:27)
11. Advance Romance (7:43)
12. Strictly Genteel (6:36)

Note: Some European releases of this album omitted *Royal March From "L'Histoire Du Soldat"* and *Theme From The Bartok Piano Concerto #3* due to concerns that the families of Stravinsky or Bartok might object to Zappa's treatment of these pieces. They didn't.

You Can't Do That On Stage Anymore, Vol. 6

Official Release #59. Originally Released: July 10, 1992

Tracklisting:

DISC 1

06. Honey, Don't You Want A Man Like Me? (4:01)
15. Make A Sex Noise (3:09)

DISC 2

05. We're Turning Again (4:56)
06. Alien Orifice (4:16)
07. Catholic Girls (4:04)
08. Crew Slut (5:33)
12. Lonesome Cowboy Nando (5:09)

Notes: The coda for *Alien Orifice* is from an unknown 88 source, but the remainder is from a 1981 performance. *Lonesome Cowboy Nando* is from the final 9 June Genoa show, intercut with a performance from 1971 featuring Jimmy Carl Black.

Trance-Fusion

Official Release #79. Released: November 7, 2006

Tracklisting:

01. Chunga's Revenge (7:01)
04. A Cold Dark Matter (3:31)
07. Scratch & Sniff (3:56)
08. Trance-Fusion (4:19)
09. Gorgo (2:41)
11. Soul Polka (3:17)
13. After Dinner Smoker (4:45)
15. Finding Higgs' Boson (3:41)
16. Bavarian Sunset (4:00)

Notes: This is an album of Zappa's 'air sculptures': *A Cold Dark Matter* is a guitar solo taken from an 88 performance of *Inca Roads*; *Scratch & Sniff* from *City Of Tiny Lites*; *Trance-Fusion* from *Marque-son's Chicken*; *Gorgo* and *After Dinner Smoker* from *The Torture Never Stops*; *Soul Polka* from *Oh No*; *Finding Higg's Boson* from *Hot Plate Heaven At The Green Hotel*; and *Bavarian Sunset* from *Loops*, a jam with Dweezil.

The Frank Zappa AAAFRNAA Birthday Bundle

Exclusive download from iTunes. Released: December 21, 2006

Tracklisting:

04. Bamboozled By Love (5:41)

Note: Unlike the material edited together by Frank, this posthumous release contains a complete performance from the 8 May Wein show.

The Frank Zappa AAAFRNAAA Birthday Bundle

Exclusive download from iTunes. Released: December 21, 2008

Tracklisting:

02. More Trouble Every Day (5:48)
05. America The Beautiful (3:35)

Note: Unlike the material edited together by Frank, this posthumous release contains complete performances from the 8 May Wein and 25 March Uniondale shows.

Beat The Boots III - Disc Two

Exclusive download from AmazonMP3 and iTunes. Released: January 25, 2009

Tracklisting:

12. I Am the Walrus (03:43)
13. America the Beautiful (03:16)

Note: This posthumously released 'official bootleg' contains complete performances of two 'Broadway' songs, from the 13 March Springfield and 12 March Burlington shows.

The FRANK ZAPPA aaafnraaaa Birthday Bundle

Exclusive download from iTunes. Released: December 21, 2010

Tracklisting:

07. My Guitar Wants To Kill Your Mama (3:34)
12. Stairway To Heaven (10:10)

Note: Unlike the material edited together by Frank, this posthumous release contains complete performances from the 21 March Syracuse and 9 March Buffalo shows.

The FRANK ZAPPA AAAFNRAAAAAM Birthday Bundle

Exclusive download from iTunes. Released: 21 December 2011

Tracklisting:

09. Peaches (Vienna 88) (2:50)

Notes: Unlike the material edited together by Frank, this posthumous release contains a complete performance from the 8 May Stadthalle show. Despite Frank singling out Ike Willis' contribution to the "1988 Deluxe Version of *Peaches En Regalia*" in *The Real Frank Zappa Book*, for reasons unknown Ike is not officially listed as one of the players on this particular rendition.

Frank Zappa For President

Official Release #105. Originally Released: July 15, 2016

Tracklisting:

05. When The Lie's So Big (3.39)
07. America The Beautiful (3.36)

Note: Unlike the material edited together by Frank, this posthumous release contains complete performances from the 25 March Uniondale show; *America The Beautiful* is as per *The Frank Zappa AAAFRNAAA Birthday Bundle* version.

Zappa '88: The Last U.S. Show

Official Release #119. Released: June 18, 2021

Tracklisting:

DISC 1

01. "We Are Doing Voter Registration Here" (7:00)
02. The Black Page - New Age Version (7:12)
03. I Ain't Got No Heart (1:59)
04. Love Of My Life (2:14)
05. Inca Roads (8:44)
06. Sharleena (6:22)
07. Who Needs The Peace Corps? (2:29)
08. I Left My Heart In San Francisco (0:35)
09. Dickie's Such An Asshole (6:01)
10. When The Lie's So Big (3:38)
11. Jesus Thinks You're A Jerk (8:47)
12. Sofa #1 (2:45)
13.   One Man, One Vote (2:35)
12. Sofa #1 (2:45)
13. One Man, One Vote (2:35)
14. Happy Birthday, Chad (1:30)
15. Packard Goose Pt. I (2:56)
16. Royal March From "L'Histoire Du Soldat" (1:17)
17. Theme From The Bartok Piano Concerto #3 (1:20)
18. Packard Goose Pt. II (2:03)
19. The Torture Never Stops Pt. I (5:09)
20. Theme From Bonanza (0:36)

DISC 2

01. Lonesome Cowboy Burt (4:59)
02. The Torture Never Stops Pt. II (7:29)
03. City Of Tiny Lites (9:21)
04. Pound For A Brown (10:56)
05. The Beatles Medley (9:19)
06. Peaches En Regalia (3:36)
07. Stairway To Heaven (10:09)
08. I Am The Walrus (3:42)
09. Whipping Post (6:09)
10. Bolero (5:30)
11. America The Beautiful (3:58)

Note: This posthumous release contains an almost complete performance from the 25 March Nassau Coliseum show. Missing are special guests Brother A West (who reprised his monologue heard on *The Best Band You Never Heard In Your Life*) and Dweezil, who joined his father on guitar during *Whipping Post* and *Stairway To Heaven*; the versions used here are instead taken from the 16 March show in Providence and the 23 March show in Towson, respectively.

ANDREW WOULD LIKE TO THANK...

Scott Parker and Andreas Smedegaard, for leading me to Ole Lysgaard and his fantastic tour snaps; Jan Lundgren for getting them to me; and Erling Agergaard for actually snapping them. Hakan Tuna, for leading me to Milo. Clint Walker and Mark McInnes, for the Ike Willis video story. Chris Opperman, for transcribing Mike Keneally's tour diaries. Pauline Butcher Bird, for her frank interview and kindness. Milo Albonico, for his amazing photographs and friendship. Reinhard Preuss, for photos and memorabilia. Mick Zeuner, for brotherly love, maps and snaps. Deepinder Cheema, for taking me on set. Fabio Treves and photographer Maki Galimberti. Jerry Bloom and Andy Bishop, for their patience. All my family and friends, though many of you will never even read this book. And finally: Frank and his amazing 1988 band, for producing fantastic music in trying circumstances.